The
Window
in the
Corner

By the same author

The Children's War: Evacuation 1939–1945

The Good Step-parents' Guide

Must Divorce the Children?

Sins of the Father (Peter Owen)

A Time to Learn (Peter Owen)

The Window in the Corner

A Half-Century of
Children's Television

Ruth Inglis

Peter Owen
London and Chester Springs

PETER OWEN PUBLISHERS
73 Kenway Road, London SW5 0RE

Peter Owen books are distributed in the USA by
Dufour Editions Inc., Chester Springs, PA 19425-0007

First published in Great Britain 2003 by Peter Owen Publishers
© Ruth Inglis 2003

ISBN 0 7206 1105 9

A catalogue record for this book is available from
the British Library

Printed and bound by
Zrinski SA, Croatia

To Maisie and Phoebe

Acknowledgements

I have spoken to a number of friends, former colleagues and television producers about their experiences and feelings about television, especially as they had viewed it as children. Some, such as Mike Batt, Jonathan Cohen, Marilyn Gaunt and Jeremy Swan, have made some stunning children's programmes in the past and some are still doing so; others merely remembered how watching television made them shiver with fright and delight as schoolchildren. They all gave me insights into the making and enjoying of this fascinating glaucous eye of images and movement, and I am hugely indebted to them:

Amanda Allsop, Mark Andresen, Mike Batt, Penelope Bennett, Virginia Biggs, Tim Brooking, Peggy Charren, Diana Clater, Lloyd Clater, Maisie Clater, Phoebe Clater, Jonathan Cohen, John Coop, Anabel Davis, Clare Dover, Gaby Fagan, Dick Foster, John Gardiner, Tracy Gardiner (now Mrs Tracy Buckley), Marilyn Gaunt, Emmie Giles, Marjorie Giles, Neil Langdon Inglis (th§is history's tireless on-line researcher), Peter Jackson (Froebel Educational Institute, Inc.), Nick Magnus, Sybil Marshall, Jane McKerron, Charlotte Metcalf, Janice Nutkins, Walter Pechenuk, Oliver Postgate, Elizabeth Ray, Jo Anne Robertson, Pauline Shaw, Monica Sims, Jeremy Swan, Rosalyn Watson, Jack White and Sylvia Woodeson.

Preface

My first glimpse of children's television, the sight of the American puppet Howdy Doody's startlingly livid red freckles in the fifties, did not really prepare me to be a historian of this medium. Still, I'm not sure there is any particular prescribed background required for the task. Children's television's fifty-year journey has been a choppy one and perhaps no specific person is perfectly suited to chart it.

Autobiographically speaking, I could be viewed as a reasonable choice for a chronicler. I arrived in Britain in 1959 just in time to look at the BBC's historic *Watch with Mother* with my four-year-old daughter. I had just been married for the second time to Granada Television presenter Brian Inglis, a marriage which lasted for thirteen years, and so I had a backstairs view of what life in a studio entailed. This included trying to help him wash off the Max Factor 'honey-peach' pancake foundation powder the make-up artists plastered over his attractive Dublin Irish features for *All Our Yesterdays*, a documentary of year-by-year wartime Britain. I also got to know some of his sociable, dashing colleagues. The light of fame bathed them all so that pub privacy came with difficulty but not merry-making.

In 1968–9 I worked for Pauline Shaw, director-producer at Granada, as a researcher–writer for a schools programme called *The*

Facts Are These, a series dealing with six social health issues. I would like to say that writing about the dangers of sexually transmitted diseases for the over-fifteens prepared me for analysing the charms of *Muffin the Mule* thirty years later, but I can't honestly say that it has (though Pauline and I did win a prize for clarity and presentation from the British Health Council).

My year's stint at Granada did reveal the exceeding kindness and modesty of those dealing with schools and children's programmes. Jack White and John Coop were down-to-earth, modest executives of the children's department. Unlike the breed who dealt with adult viewers, I thought they had their priorities solidly in place; very much less ego, less preening (in fact, none). What counted were the children. The many children's television performers, producers and composers I have interviewed for this book all seem to possess this modesty and dedication. This is not to say that they idealize children in a late Victorian, early Edwardian sentimental way. But they tend to give them two most valuable contributions – honesty and respect.

Children's television is a slightly curious field. Of all entertainments, it is probably the most ambivalent in nature. Children usually love it, both the good and the bad material, while parents and even its producers have never been totally convinced of its value. Does it teach? Does it corrupt? Is it harmless? Is it beneficial? The soul-searching goes on and on. It must be the only medium that has thrown its creators into fits of despair even when it becomes a huge success (as happened with BBC director Edward Barnes, when *Grange Hill*, the realistic long-running drama involving secondary-school children, became a matter of controversy in the early nineties, particularly for its depiction of sexuality).

Even today child experts are undecided abut the effects of children's viewing. While ten years ago psychiatrists were almost sure that television could unlock dark urges in the young, provoking imitative violence, now some of the most respected paediatricians say that dark-thoughts *can* be aroused without necessarily being acted upon. And hasn't the best children's literature always created a wide range of emotions in children?

I've tried to describe the British (and many American) winners, the 'stars' of each decade over the past half-century, but I have no doubt that many people in their middle years will say I have left out a crucial programme or two that they favoured. If this is so, I apologize. I have tried to concentrate on programmes that have moved children's television forward in a new direction (Oliver Postgate's *The Clangers* towards the surreal; Anne Wood's *Teletubbies* to entertainment for a much younger viewer; and so on). The danger of enumerating them all is the risk inherent in any list-making – that of incurring indigestion and blurred vision.

My history has not included video games (so no illustrations of the delectable Lara Croft). Video games did not really emerge in strength until the very end of the twentieth century, and I have been keen to stay within the fifty-year time frame. With such a rich diet, this seemed only fair.

The happiest part of writing this history is that I became aware that, especially with regard to the art of animation, children's television has managed to get better and better. I'm not going to mourn the demise of the big, wooden, faintly maligned Howdy Doody, for example, when the tapping, rhythmic Tweenies are around or noble Bob the Builder or even the pouting, giggling Tubbies. I will even forgive Barney, that saccharine dinosaur, for being such a goody-goody. In this age we need do-gooders who ask us to mind our manners.

Contents

Illustrations

between pages 128 and 129

Child actors taking school classes in an improvised classroom at the BBC's Lime Grove Studios, 1952

Lord Reith, Director-General of the BBC, with Dorothea Brooking, head of Children's Drama, 1952

Andy Pandy and Teddy, created in the fifties for the BBC's *Watch With Mother* series

Dorothea Brooking, acting as producer of *Meet the Penguins*, pictured with animator Bill Hooper in the fifties

Bill and Ben, the Flowerpot Men, with Little Weed in the original *Watch With Mother* series from the fifties

The BBC's *Blue Peter* presenters Peter Purves, Valerie Singleton and John Noakes, who worked together in the late sixties and early seventies

Valerie Singleton in Hong Kong wearing her *Blue Peter* badge in the early seventies

Patrick Troughton in the role of the second *Dr Who*

The fire brigade of *Trumpton* at the village clocktower

Magpie presenters Mick Robertson, Douglas Rae and Susan Stranks, 1972

Oliver Postgate with *Bagpuss* in the studio, 1974

Dorothea Brooking during rehearsals of an adaption of Rumer Godden's *The Diddakoi*, called *Kizzy,* at Lime Grove Studios, 1976

Dorothea Brooking and Monica Sims, head of BBC's Children's Programmes, with John Craven at the Pye Colour Television Awards in 1980

Todd Carty and Terry Siu Patt, the two rascally schoolboys who starred in *Grange Hill*

The British-made cartoon *Dangermouse*, a success on both sides of the Atlantic during the eighties

Characters from *The Wind in the Willows,* created for commercial television by Mark Hall and Brian Cosgrove in the eighties

The popular *Bob the Builder*, created by Peter Acton in the late eighties

The Tweenies, the BBC's big success story of the late nineties

Jeremy Swan directing *Sooty Heights* in 1999

American creation Barney, the purple dinosaur

A young Kosovar refugee with a Tellytubby doll *en route* home to his war-ravaged country

1
Early Years

When children's television first began in Britain two years after the war ended in May 1945 it was a tentative, low-key affair. There was a feeling in the BBC at that time, fostered by Lord Reith, its first Director-General, that children deserved a small televisual treat, a time slot of their own on the new media, which at first was only a tiddler in the broadcasting empire in any case. So, in 1947, children's television was a small, kindly offering from a relatively minor medium. Radio was still king at the time, its wartime role as the crucial news information-giver continuing to be deeply cherished nationwide.

Lord Reith was an austere giant, well over six foot tall. He held powerful Scottish Presbyterian views on how people should behave, ruling the BBC with a zealous missionary fervour and an impressive integrity of spirit. He approached the prospect of entertaining children with characteristic austerity. This was to be simple, straightforward, nursery-style entertainment, wholesome and gently humorous. The budget was as modest as its aims. When the Children's Department became an official branch of the Corporation in 1951 there were only seven producers on the children's programming roster. None of the producers had any formal broadcasting experience, but they appeared to be naturals. Fortunately, they brought verve and enthusiasm along with their inexperience and a willingness to participate in all activities – furniture-moving, a little amateur carpentry, room-hopping. A compartmentalizing, union-oriented division of tasks and description of what was job-appropriate or inappropriate came much later.

The late Dorothea Brooking, for instance, an early producer who pioneered the television filming of such serial classics as Frances Hodgson Burnett's *The Secret Garden*, E. Nesbit's *Five Children and It* and Noel Streatfeild's *Thursday's Child*, was virtually a one-woman band, according to her son, Tim. She made her own story-boards for each production (and later for *Play School*). This was very much a separate artist's job later on, but she enjoyed fashioning her own scenes down to the last kitchen or flower garden and set her fine stamp on each production, ignoring any criticisms from the 'suits' of the day. Tim Brooking says that she found frustrations and put-downs in this male-dominated field but forged ahead, seemingly undaunted.

There was very much a compassionate, 'suffer the little children' atmosphere abroad in the immediate post-war broadcasting service. In so far as those in control of the BBC pondered the psyche of British children at all – which was doubtful, as only in isolated Hampstead in north London, viewed as a precious islet with specialized interests in child psychiatry, was this at all common – Lord Reith and his subalterns felt the need to shelter and heal the young.

Children in wartime had had a rotten time of it – with some 3 million children being parted from their parents in monumental evacuation waves over the five and a half years of war. Now they thought to need reassuring and soothing with the aid of puppets, marionettes, teddy bears and soft strokings of piano keys. Nothing shattering. The more abrasive animation of the Disney kingdom across the Atlantic, of cat fights and wily, stroppy mice, was not for British children. (Disney did not come to commercial television until the late fifties and, contrary to the early BBC's expectations, proved to be astonishingly successful.)

It was not surprising that the use of puppets and marionettes was seized upon as the best entertainment for children in these early years (and for puppet-driven television they were mainly thinking of child viewers of four to eight years old). The dramatizing of children's classics was designed for eight- to eleven-year olds and also considered restful fare.

The use of the ancient art of puppetry fitted in admirably with the predominant belief that children required gentle, calming entertainment ('not the thump, thump, thump' of US cartoons, as one producer put it). There was a need for tranquil programming for these possibly traumatized youngsters who had trembled beneath the onslaught of the Flying Bombs, the 'Doodlebugs' of 1944, and perhaps seen their homes destroyed, fathers disappear for ever, went the thinking.

A cynic might also suggest that puppetry and 'made for television' classics were more economical than original, complex series, and certainly, then as now, budgets ruled and children's programming was allocated the least funds. (The rise and rise of the economic success of children's television has been one of the most startling of metamorphoses to have occurred in this area of entertainment in the past fifty years: the redoubtable pre-school serial, *Teletubbies*, for example, is the BBC's current No. 1 best-seller, with £12 billion grossed annually from its international sales.)

The first cosy offering in the BBC's 'protective vein' of projects came in 1947 with *Muffin the Mule*; Annette Mills, Sir John's late sister, was the pianist and 'diseuse', and Ann Hogarth was the puppeteer. This charming black-and-white wooden mule was pulled by the traditional six or more puppet strings and clattered across a piano top to 'whisper' to Annette Mills about village gossip and the doings of other animal puppets. She would repeat his whispered secrets in a pleasant, easy manner, obviating the need for a ventriloquist, possibly another

19

budgetary saving (the upright piano used was the only piano the BBC had at the time, its props being minimal).

Muffin the Mule was hardly high drama, but it did capture the then modest viewing audience of the time (only a third of the population had television sets, and these were very small, just nine inches in diameter). But Muffin's child audiences were appreciative. A 62-year-old writer friend told me how excited she would become at the prospect of seeing Muffin. 'I was about six and used to wait breathlessly for the sound of his clattering heels,' she told me, 'as if he were a pair of castanets shaped like a mule. I found the sound very comforting, though I had to steal over to a neighbour's house to see the programme. My parents disapproved.'

Another puppet that caught the post-war child's imagination, rivalling Muffin the Mule in popularity, was a small white bear with black ears and a black nose called Sooty. His creator was the late Harry Corbett, a part-time magician. Sooty was a glove-puppet that Harry had found in a North Pier novelty shop on holiday with his family in Blackpool.

Sooty first appeared in the BBC children's series *Saturday Special* in 1952. He was a mischievous bear, and the idea was that he lived up a chimney most of the time and that the blackened ears and nose came from his chimney-sweeping activities. He was keen on dousing Harry's face with ink or flour, and part of his appeal came from his ability to put one over on Harry with his cheekiness (the bear also liked to bash him on the head with a balsa-wood hammer). Harry's grimacing face as he was trounced and humiliated by his bear was the high point of the drama, and children came to delight in Harry's defeat and crestfallen last words: 'Bye-bye, everybody. Bye-bye . . .'

Sooty became a national favourite because of this general irreverence – squirting people indiscriminately with his water pistol (even dousing Prince Philip at a trade fair). This was the period when the Royal Family seemed to be quite regularly involved in BBC pro-

grammes and not just at Christmas: the squirting of Prince Phil
forgiven because the young Princess Anne was reported to be a huge
fan of Sooty's. (In 1958, for example, Prince Charles and Princess
Anne visited the BBC set that starred the parrot Cocky the Cockatoo
on David Attenborough's magazine programme, *Studio E*.)

In 1957 Sweep, a sausage-eating dog, joined Sooty and amused the
nation by carting around a huge supply of bones. The humour that
Harry Corbett generated with his puppets was predicated on the gentle assumption that he was really a bit of a victim of his own toy
creations' pranks. His mobile, rubbery face shown being splashed or
stained by small, fuzzy animals delighted young viewers (the television
spin-off merchandising which has grown vastly and globally over the
years perhaps first came into being around this time: in the mid-fifties
the *Daily Mirror* published a Sooty annual with the bear pictured playing his xylophone on the cover).

Sooty and Harry Corbett were long-lasting favourites on the
BBC's children's schedule and were kept on until 1967 when they
were axed with the arrival of a new Controller of BBC 1, Paul Fox.
However, the axeing was not fatal – Sooty and Corbett were signed up
quickly by Thames Television and lasted until 1992 (and a new series
with Sooty acting as an occasional hotelier began in 2000 under the
artistic direction of Jeremy Swan).

In the USA another puppet, bigger than Muffin but still wooden
and operated by visible strings, Howdy Doody, was captivating thousands of small American viewers. I used to watch his freckled wooden
countenance and bulging blue eyes over the heads of my kindergarten-aged niece and nephew in Boston when baby-sitting. I always
found his red freckles and shiny countenance a mite sinister, his lippy
smile a little vulpine. He was on the screen from 1947 to 1960. There
were estimated to be 180,000 television sets in the USA when Howdy
Doody made his début in 1947, and his popularity was such that,
according to one writer, the reaction to the show's singsong theme,

'It's Howdy Doody Time', was 'positively Pavlovian'.[1] This cowboy puppet, with his gingham neckerchief, cowboy boots and spurs, came from 'Doodyville', a possibly scatological reference (as in former President George Bush's oft-quoted 'deep doo doo' phrase) which may have foreshadowed the much more obvious scatology of *South Park*, the nineties' black-edged, satirical animation series.

The popularity of Howdy Doody, the creation of Bob Smith, spiralled into near national madness, viewed by both children and their parents, during the run-up to the presidential election of 1948. The puppet was embraced as a presidential candidate, and the show's studio bosses received 60,000 requests for 'Howdy Doody for President' campaign buttons. Harry S. Truman won instead, though some wags remarked that Howdy Doody was hardly less cornpone in manner than the victor from Missouri.

The hoop-la surrounding Howdy Doody did not reach Britain, but the popularity of television was almost as heated. The fact that only a third of the population in the UK possessed sets had less to do with licensing laws than with the restricted use of transmission sites. Parts of Wiltshire were deprived of them, to judge by the following complaint published in the 'Letters to the Editor' column of the *Daily Express* on 15 December 1952:

I'm One of Britain's Pitied People . . . No Television for Us!
I am one of Britain's social outsiders. I live in a backward area. We have not yet got television. We fall between two stations. TV is to the right of us. TV is to the left of us . . . and the promise of TV tomorrow. But seeing is much more than believing.

I and my neighbours exist in a kind of cultural blindness, humiliated by inability to understand references to (for instance) *What's My Line?*

And what a gulf divides Children's Hour fans from the eye-witnesses of Andy Pandy and Muffin the Mule!

Even at boarding-school our children have to live down the shame of coming from a district not privileged with TV.

Those who live beside a TV set are so maddeningly superior!

If they come slumming into our neighbourhood and we happen to mention a radio programme which we specially enjoy, they smile tolerantly as if we were a museum-piece confessing to a liking for silent films.

Friends proudly display their TV sets as if they themselves had personally invented the modern miracle.

And oh how pressingly they insist that we lack not having our fill of TV before we return to our distressed areas. There is indeed a sound barrier rising between those districts with TV and those without. Are the bureaucrats, with their love of standardisation, aware of the increasing danger of a generation growing up who do not speak the same language or see the same way as their contemporaries on the other side of the country?

Yes, it is imperative that TV should quickly be brought within the range of every district of Great Britain. Even if it is only for the satisfaction of declaring that TV is 'tripe' and we would not dream of buying a set!

(Mrs) M.I. Maidment,
Vale House, St Ann Street, Salisbury

Londoners were much more fortunate *vis-à-vis* television transmission, and the South-East, then as now, tended to have blanket coverage of the latest offerings. Judging from the news items of the day, television, when available as it was in the urban areas, was cheaply and readily supplied by local councils. A report in the *Daily Express* on 7 July 1950, headed 'Television for 2 Shillings Weekly', announced that Hammersmith Council tenants could have television sets installed in their living rooms for an installation charge of 10 shillings (50 pence) and a weekly payment of 2 shillings. For the first year, the news item revealed, the Council would pay for the receiving licences. This is certainly a long way from today's television licence charge of an annual £104.[2]

Television was becoming cheap and increasingly visible in even the humblest homes by the late fifties. But it still wasn't regarded as the compulsive fare it is today, with such crowd-pullers as *EastEnders* or *The Simpsons,* the US animated series depicting the deliciously dysfunctional American family which delights both young and old.

Nor could television compete with a live show then as it does today (witness the thousands who preferred to watch the year 2000 arrive over the Thames on their sets rather than from Embankment pavements). Audiences preferred their talent live then, and Frank Sinatra, Judy Garland or Frankie Vaughan could pack the music-halls to the gunwales. Even to see Elvis Presley on the movie screen produced a frisson among teenagers. On 6 October 1958 the newspapers reported hundreds of teenagers rioting at an Elvis Presley film, *King Creole,* which was playing at the Astoria Cinema in the Old Kent Road in south-east London. The teenagers slashed forty cinema seats to pieces and threw the mounds of stuffing on to the stage. No reason was given for the noisy vandalism. The New Orleans beat raised pulses, it seemed.

For the BBC such shenanigans had no place or interest, however, and if the post-war world became a bit wild socially as the decade of the fifties progressed, this did not (at least until the ratings proved in 1958 that competition was becoming savage) ruffle the programme-makers, especially not during the reign of Freda Lingstrom, head of Children's Programmmes from 1951 to 1956. She was a stout, middle-aged woman of impeccable taste and a strong feeling that children should be protected from television dross of any kind. She disapproved of children's programmes that seemed cacophonous, showy or formulaic. She detested Enid Blyton for the predictable adventures of her Famous Five and wouldn't give her creations house room. (Ironically,

Donald Baverstock, Blyton's son-in-law, became Assistant Co
of Programmes in the early sixties, but by that time she had left

Children's television prospered under Freda Lingstrom's tough, unyielding reign. She fought her corner with admirable fortitude, revealing particular displeasure when she felt that adult subjects were encroaching on her children's programming time. The transition between children's times and adult viewing seems to have given the producers a particular headache, which they tried to overcome with incongruous and meaningless inserts on agriculture and similar subjects. Freda Lingstrom grew especially fierce when the BBC planners inserted a special on 'apple growers' after a children's programme. Why would a child be interested in apple production? she asked a male colleague crossly. There was no talk of the 'glass ceiling' in Freda Lingstrom's day, but it is clear that she hit her head on its vitreous surface many times. Her male colleagues knuckled under her rule, surprisingly, but made fun of her behind her back, calling her 'the Old Cough Drop'.

Freda Lingstrom's vision of what children's television should be was very Reithian, protective and strait-laced; it was, metaphorically speaking, rather like handing children comforting cups of hot chocolate at regular, carefully timed intervals. Nothing, said Lingstrom, was to be 'frightening, cruel or vulgar'. Above all, it was not to be American. She would screen Westerns only 'over her dead body', she declared, and this animus was also directed at US cartoons. She subscribed to the views expressed by Mary Adams, the Corporation's head of Television Talks, who wrote in a company memorandum of 1950 that 'children's viewing will be encouraged in the interests of programme quality', adding that 'children's encounters with it [the television set] had to be both rationed and planned'.[3] She added that parents should be co-opted into the viewing, ensuring that their offspring would be duly controlled by their authority (a hopeful expectation which has been repeatedly expressed by television monitoring heads – with uniformly disappointing results – for the past half-century, human behaviour having changed less than the technological wonders of the viewing screen apparently).

Freda Lingstrom stated that she deplored the 'viewing habit' in children, a curious prejudice in a programme-maker. This dislike, or even fear, of children's dependency on the medium made for an odd outcome: children were allowed only to have a 'little piece of time' for their entertainment. The post-war habit of rationing had invaded all areas, it seemed.

Fortunately, Lingstrom approved of the classics; thus respected authors' works were given her stamp of approval during the highly productive five years of her leadership. One great hit of her reign was *Billy Bunter*. He was the fat, eponymous hero of *Billy Bunter of Greyfriars School*, written by Frank Richards in the early part of the twentieth century and serialized in a weekly magazine called *The Magnet*.

Billy Bunter was 'the fat boy of the Remove' at a typical rural public school where tuck boxes, severe masters, stodgy prefects and unbendable house rules prevailed. The role was beautifully played by Gerald Campion. His vast abdomen, small round eye-glasses, pastry-covered fingers, ridiculous fringe and cap made a farce out of public school behaviour and dress regulations. Kynaston Reeves, who played his straight-faced, purse-lipped master Dr Quelch, was the perfect foil for Bunter's buffoonery. Bunter's catchphrases were universally adored and repeated: 'Crickey!', 'Beasts!' and 'I say, you fellows!' An unexpected bonus for the show's producers was the huge addition of adult viewers who hurried home from the office to see the second showing of the programme (it was transmitted at 5.45 p.m. for children and then two hours later for adults). These unexpected ratings boosters were fathers (usually), former passionate readers of Bunter stories in *The Magnet*.

Lingstrom's emphasis on adapting the classics helped pave the way for what many television chroniclers called 'the Golden Age of television'. It did not seem to matter that the children's team had only one studio to screen in at Lime Grove and three cameras to roll on to the studio floor. Lingstrom and Dorothea Brooking, children's drama head, formed a tireless, dedicated duo, and in spite of their tight budgets and limited space and equipment they produced some stunning serials.

The Railway Children, by E. Nesbit, was the first of them, made in 1951. On the few outdoor location shots the young actors froze in their cotton clothes during the winter shoot (the series was aired in March 1951 but shot over the winter). Marian Chapman played the heroine, Bobby, the part taken on more famously by Jenny Agutter in the BBC's 1968 production.

The series, based on the story of the struggles of an impoverished and fatherless family in late Victorian times, struck a strong chord with its post-war audiences, accustomed to the recent wartime spectacle of fatherless families and courageous lone mothers. The show was filmed twice a week, once midweek and again on Sunday afternoons.

It became a crowd-puller on Sundays, as did Brooking's subsequent filmed classics, Frances Hodgson Burnett's *The Secret Garden* in 1952 (starring Elizabeth Saunders as the heroine Mary Lennox) and her adaptation of Rumer Godden's *The Diddakoi,* called *Kizzy* in the serial, which features a young half-gypsy girl.

Dorothea Brooking continued to work miracles with little financial backing. In *The Secret Garden* she triumphed again by finding a real walled garden near the studio to match the one described in Burnett's classic, thus injecting reality into the tale of three lonely children in Yorkshire who find companionship and magic in the discovery of a hidden walled garden.

Watch With Mother was for the young child, aged six or under, and a 'little piece of time' was indeed just what this age group acquired. On a typical day, for example, on 20 January 1954, the children were allotted fifteen minutes of *The Woodentops*.[4] This was followed by a closedown until 5 p.m. when older children, aged six to sixteen, were offered programmes, each of about fifteen minutes' duration, one called *The Outdoors* and the other *Stories of the Piano*. From 6 to 7 p.m. there was a complete closedown, and this blackout was named 'the Toddler's Truce'.

In the early years all these programmes, produced in one studio in Alexandra Palace, north London, were hampered by lack of space, equipment and trained personnel. The BBC moved to Lime Grove, west London, at around the time of the Coronation in 1953, but it took its diminished facilities with it.

The one asset that enriched the service was the attractive, stylish, silver-tongued male presenters who became television icons over the following decades: Huw Wheldon, Tony Hart, Richard Dimbleby, Cliff Michelmore and David Attenborough, to name a few. Presenters were needed to fill the time gaps between programmes – a prosaic start. As is so often the case with new ventures, the camaraderie and excitement of a new medium and fresh material imbued these presenters with an exuberant, almost knockabout air. Anna Home, in her autobiography, tells of how, when presenting a children's programme on hobbies called *All Your Own*, Huw Wheldon absent-mindedly leant on a model harpsichord made by a child out of matchsticks, crushing it to bits. Unabashed, he told the child breezily: 'Oh well, I'm sure you can put it back together again.'

Considering the paradoxical position in which Freda Lingstrom found herself – producing children's material that she felt should be rationed, as if she were dealing in dentally unsound toffees – her programmes were very successful, at least initially (she had, it should be remembered, no competition whatsoever). Perhaps more surprising is that the eighties' reissue of a *Watch With Mother* video became such a major success.[5] But nostalgia for a perceived 'golden age' of television seems to be even more intense than ever. Adults evidently yearn for the 'feelgood factor' induced by programmes recalled from their childhoods. When the BBC destroyed three-quarters of its film and video archives in the seventies they had no conception of the rolls of cash they were almost literally burning along with the celluloid spools.[6] Watching the reissue of the BBC's *The Best of Watch With Mother* recently, I wondered if it shouldn't be called *The Best of What's Left of Watch With Mother*. Certainly I recall more entertaining programmes in this series during the late fifties when I first came to London and watched them with my five-year-old daughter.

Watch With Mother, a combination of three children's series, was launched in the early fifties and was Freda Lingstrom's memorable introduction and contribution to children's television. The series was a first in a very important way – the first seriously planned combination of entertainment and education for a specific age group (the under-sixes). In a sense it was the progenitor of the most effective 'fun-cum-learning' programmes of the future: *Sesame Street* and *Teletubbies*. (The latter does have an early learning pattern, too, though a less recognizable one, designed as it is for toddlers aged two to four and relying for learning on repetition and familiar, expected routines and happenings.)

Though *Watch With Mother* was launched in its final form in 1954, *Andy Pandy* preceded the series, first seen on 11 July 1950. Andy Pandy was a wide-eyed toddler in a striped romper suit and a Tyrolean hat who lived in a picnic basket. He appeared by himself initially and was later joined by a battered-looking Teddy and a rag doll called Looby Loo.

Watching the re-release of the series, I charted the educational content of *Andy Pandy*: there were rhymes, songs, a voice-over describing Andy Pandy's tricycle in some detail and a bit of rhythmic fun concerning the cycle's bell ('Ting-a-ling, ting-a-ling, you can hear his bell ring'). As creaky and old-fashioned as it seemed, even though now souped up with colour, the educational content was obvious: the description of objects; the allying of objects to accompanying verse and melody; the invitation to move to music in unison ('Join in, children, jump in the air when Teddy does,' etc.).

Dedicated and talented people joined the small production staff: opera singer Gladys Whitred sang the songs and puppeteer Molly Gibson pulled the strings. Only twenty-six original black-and-white episodes were made and were seen over and over again. In 1970 thirteen new episodes were made in colour. Initially, the show was transmitted on Tuesdays at 3.45 p.m. for fifteen minutes.

In 1952 *The Flowerpot Men* was added to *Watch With Mother* on Wednesdays. Bill and Ben were identical puppets and were made out of flowerpots, their hands out of gardening gloves, and there were small hobnail boots on their feet. Their communication skills were their oddest characteristic: they spoke a kind of 'flibadob' and 'flabadob' language. They lived in two huge flowerpots behind a potting shed, and the central action came when they peered over the parapets of their pots to 'chat' when the gardener went home for lunch. Their neighbour, Little Weed, who possessed a strangled violin E-string kind of voice, would alert them to the (presumably) dangerous return of the gardener. In the episode I saw recently, Bill and Ben hoisted themselves out of their jars and danced a puppet's jig on the ice that had formed in their garden, creaking back when they were alerted by Little Weed to the gardener's return.

Its appeal to young children is simple and perhaps self-evident. The Flowerpot Men, like many pre-school children, speak their own secret gobbledygook (the Teletubbies also have their own unintelligible 'gang' parlance of giggles and coos); they have a secret place and hide from the gardener, the Universal Adult figure. The Flowerpot Men live a life of 'hide and seek', one of the most loved of children's games, a teasing 'trick' on adults.

The final offering of this trilogy was *The Woodentops*, which arrived in 1955 in the Friday afternoon slot. It was peopled with eight tiny puppets with little round heads: Daddy and Mummy Woodentop, their baby and twin four-year-olds and Mr and Mrs Scrubbit, the daily cleaning woman and her husband. There were also minor characters such as their gardener Sam, Buttercup the cow and a roguish canine called Spotty Dog. It was one of the most popular children's shows to issue from the Lime Grove studio.

Viewers today, especially adults, are confounded or irritated by *The Woodentops*. 'Look at its horrible gender-role stereotyping,' one young tour guide whispered to me at the 1998–2000 Imperial War Museum's exhibition 'From the Bomb to the Beatles'. 'Mrs Woodentop is ironing so proudly,' she fumed. 'I wonder why she didn't use Mrs Scrubbit?' commented an older woman with a touch of longing. Viewers in the fifties seemed to enjoy this happy family, and certainly its middle-class tone and apathetic approach to women's designated roles in life were uncontroversial at the time (as Betty Friedan points out in *The Feminine Mystique*,[7] women were in love with their kitchens in the fifties). And whatever else was going on, the Woodentop family was involved in the serious under-the-surface task of educating pre-school and primary school children. In the episode I saw, the Woodentop twins count as Mr Scrubbit stands on his hands to amuse them. The stilted playtime activities of the Woodentops were not, we can be sure, as important to its makers as the fact the young children were learning to count and acquire other skills, and being amused into the bargain. Such was the two-pronged aim of all these entertainments.

Lingstrom had every reason to be proud of her daily afternoon slot of *Watch With Mother*. The series kept up a very high standard of excellence and freedom from commercialism. This high-powered woman director was so anti-brand name that even the word 'Hoover' was strictly banned from use and 'vacuum cleaner' a compulsory substitute.

The programmes encouraged fantasy and curiosity in children.

Rag, Tag and Bobtail, added in 1953 and based on the stories of Louise Cochrane, featured three woodland creatures, a hedgehog, a mouse and a rabbit, and obviously encouraged both compassion for 'all creatures great and small' and a possible zoological, scientific bent in pre-schoolers as well.

Horticultural interest was also soon stimulated with the introduction of *The Herbs*, which consisted of a curious assortment of people and animals sporting herbal titles: Dill the dog, Lady Rosemary, the Chives family, Sir Basil and the eventual star turn, Parsley the Lion, who went on to have his own spin-off series in the sixties. (I have met several zealous women cooks in their late forties who swear that they became interested in growing herbs and cooking with them because of their early passion for *The Herbs*.)

Saturdays were a different matter in the eyes of the BBC programme-makers. The element of learning could be down-played, they felt, since children were off school and could be allowed to feast on variety entertainment filled with straightforward, one-act pieces.

Whirligig was the first of the Saturday treats, aired in the afternoons at the beginning of the fifties. It featured characters which could have leapt from the screens of any US Western, though they were the puppet creations of Englishman Francis Coudrill. There was Hank the Cowboy and his buck-toothed horse Silver King, along with Mexican Pete, who performed a Mexican Hat Dance.

Another great stooge to rival Harry Corbett appeared on *Whirligig*. This was Humphrey Lestocq, known as HL, who was frequently the hapless butt of his string puppet, Mr Turnip. Turnip was a rather repellent little marionette with raised eyebrows, bulging eyes and a springy topknot. HL's catchphrases were repeated all over the nation at the time: 'Goody, goody gumdrops' and 'Looky Lum'. Steve Race added to the gaiety by tickling the ivories, and Rolf Harris made his début on television with Willoughby, an easel that sprang to life.

Weekend variety shows became a forcing ground that launched

apparently timeless male performers. This was particularly true in the case of *Crackerjack!*, which first appeared in 1955, airing on Friday nights at 'five to five'. The list of *Crackerjack!* presenters resembles a BBC Hall of Fame: Eamonn Andrews, Ronnie Corbett and Leslie Crowther.

The game 'Double or Drop' featured on the programme was a zany quiz in which young participants were handed a prize if they answered a question correctly and large cabbage if they got a wrong answer. They lost if they dropped the accumulating bundle in their arms. Books, puzzles and paintboxes were awarded to the winners, but nothing was as valued as a *Crackerjack!* pencil.

Just as the variety shows became a bit zanier in the late fifties, so did the animations. The quirkiest character to come to the screen in 1957–8 was the rotund Captain Pugwash, creation of author-artist John Ryan. All the characters in this show were voiced by Peter Hawkins, who was also the voice of *The Flowerpot Men* and later of *Dr Who*'s Daleks. The animation was basic, and speech was simulated by moving a piece of card behind the various characters' open mouths. The action came from the clashes between the simple, pot-bellied, good-natured Captain and his sinister foes, Cut-throat Jake of the *Flying Dustbin* being the most malevolent.

Some grown-ups have claimed to recall naughty *double entendre* in *Captain Pugwash*. For instance, Victor Lewis-Smith, now the London *Evening Standard*'s television critic, maintained that one of the naval officers was called Master Bates. But John Ryan has strongly protested his innocence, insisting that the seaman in question was named Master Mate and that the other characters had equally innocent names. Perhaps we should leave such debates to the internet fanatics – web sites are fertile ground for such controversies and urban myths about past programme content.

During the fifties puppets such as Andy Pandy were wired very obviously from above. Things began to change at the end of the decade, however, with the arrival of Gerry Anderson, later to become the famous creator of *Thunderbirds* (see Chapter 2). Roberta Leigh, another famous animator and composer of the time, hired Gerry to make some puppet programmes. Conventional puppets did not excite his imagination, but he was out of work and desperate, so he took the job. He and his colleagues made films with a meagre £500 capital, using a run-down warehouse in Slough as a studio. They laboured and experimented until they perfected puppet animation by creating Supermarionation, which used electronic lip-synchronization and accompanying eye movement. Their efforts appear crude today, but they were a giant step forward for children's animation at the time.

Anderson's first foray into Supermarionation came with *The Adventures of Twizzle* in 1956, based on a Roberta Leigh story. Twizzle was a boy doll whose neat trick was an ability to extend his arms and legs to enormous lengths. He was joined by Footso, a small black cat with big paws, and they built a town called Stray Town, where all stray toys could get together and live in peace.

His second series, *Torchy the Battery Boy*, aired in 1957 after fifty-two episodes of *Twizzle* had been shown. Torchy was a wind-up clockwork toy who lived in Topsy-Turvy Land, where toys could walk and animals talk and the fields were strewn with lollipops and cream-buns grew on trees. This paradise for neglected toys was sometimes exchanged for less happy periods on earth when the toys became silent and unmoving and Torchy himself was bossed around by an unpleasant little girl called Bossy Boots.

With *Torchy* Anderson moved a long way from the old-fashioned practice of puppeteers behind curtains pulling strings (as apparent in *Muffin the Mule*). Torchy had moving eyes and a mobile mouth, and plastic wood was used for his head. The strings operating his mouth were finer so they would not be visible, and a soft leather strip was placed under his mouth to enable it to open and close smoothly. The puppets spoke when a wire snapped their mouths open and a spring snapped them shut again, and it was essential that this manoeuvre be concealed from viewers. Anderson was a stickler for verisimilitude.

In the four years of her rule, Freda Lingstrom had just cause for pride in the popularity of her *Watch With Mother* series. However, at the end of her reign she came in for a nasty shock with the arrival of powerful competition. ITV had begun transmitting programmes in 1955, but these screenings appeared to offer no threat at first. The commercial company's own children's programmes were dull, their national transmission patchy and their thrust a sort of dull copy of the public service fare that the BBC had initiated. They also lacked the professionalism and occasional original sparkle of the Lingstrom products.

Serious competition from commercial television arrived with Lew Grade's Associated Television production of *Robin Hood*, starring the handsome matinée idol Richard Greene. This series ran from 1955 to 1958, and though it pioneered some new film techniques its production values left something to be desired. The chain-mail tunics that the rebel hero, Robin, and his merry men wore were made of knotted string sprayed with silver paint. Shot at Nettlefold Studios, Walton-on-Thames, the sets were built on trolleys and speedily switched around to be filmed from different angles to give variety. The film unit was able to change an entire set in six minutes and turn out a 26-minute programme every four and a half days. Sherwood Forest consisted of two movable, painted wooden trees, again made to be whirled around the studio floor to give the illusion of boskiness.

The actors were a miracle of glitter and talent and future fame: among them were Thora Hird, Leo McKern, Patrick Troughton and Paul Eddington. *Watch With Mother*, for all its charm, had not offered much scope for acting talent, and even the BBC drama serials had been too low budget to splurge on an abundance of actors. Lew Grade's ATV can be praised, in retrospect, for opening the doors to talent, string vests, two trees and all!

While she was widely praised, not everyone applauded Lingstrom's efforts. Cecil McGivern, acting head of the Children's Department, wrote her the following memo in 1954, revealing a growing distaste for what he considered to be flat and unimaginative programming:

> My Dear Freda – I am afraid it was my interest in the television
> service, not my interest in the programmes, which kept me viewing
> to the end of the transmission on Sunday . . . I found this – and I
> am certain they did too – a very unexcited and unexciting viewing
> for the majority of children.[8]

The BBC came under further pressure in 1956 when ITV began importing some arresting American fare, which was slick and nowhere near as tasteless as many at the Corporation had rather superciliously considered it to be: stirring adventure serials, brisk Westerns, cartoons (*Popeye*), cowboy characters (Hopalong Cassidy) and Lassie (a beautiful collie – or a series of collies – whose whimper when attempting to alert her masters to danger was a heart-stopper, as I remember nostalgically). The viewing figures for children's television on the two rival channels changed dramatically in less than two years.[9] When considering these statistics it should of course be borne in mind that, over the period, increasingly greater numbers of viewers across the country were able to get a choice of two channels.

In 1956 the ratio of viewers in London watching the BBC compared to ITV in the first quarter of the year was 50:50; for the second quarter in London and the Midlands 40:60; for the third quarter in London, the Midlands and the North 34:66; and for the fourth quarter in London, the Midlands and the North 26:74. In the following year, 1957, the figures for the first quarter in London, the Midlands and the North were 28:72, while for the second quarter they were 30:70.

The news that ITV was attracting three times more child viewers to its channel than the BBC sent shock waves through the Corporation (panicking at ratings is not a new phenomenon).

Freda Lingstrom left the BBC in 1956, and there followed a period of general disenchantment, even cynicism, with children's television. During the last years of the fifties much less attention was devoted to children's needs, likes and dislikes. Such was the end-of-decade doldrums that the section title 'Children's Television' was dropped from the 1959 issues of the *Radio Times*. The Sunday 'Family Viewing' slot gave way to adult viewing unannounced, and *Oliver Twist* was broadcast in 1962 without the advance warnings of the violence it contained that we would expect today (Bill Sykes beating Nancy's head in, for instance). Parents reported their children having nightmares.

Fortunately, the disillusion and apathy did not drag on, and within a few years the competition did have the effect of gingering up the BBC's Children's Department. By the early to mid-sixties the Corporation was screening original programmes, both of a documentary or magazine type (such as *Blue Peter*) and new animated fantasies, which sometimes bordered on the surreal, such as *The Clangers*. Who in the cautious black-and-white fifties would have imagined the BBC offering child viewers a series like *The Clangers*, by Oliver Postgate and Peter Firmin, which featured snout-nosed creatures in pink knitted suits who lived on the moon and whose speech consisted entirely of whistles? The arrival of colour was a big part of the excitement, but, more significantly, wartime inhibitions were falling away. It was about time.

2
The Sixties

Kindly Aunty Beeb and the Sci-Fi Explosion

The BBC executives might have been discouraged by their children's television output in the late fifties and their young public's lukewarm response to it, but this was unnecessarily pessimistic of them. An extraordinary flowering of children's television was on the way, a blooming that grew, curiously enough, with the advance of technology. This is not always the case, as social history can attest. Sometimes abysmal-quality creations can emanate from state-of-the-art studios, as we are witnessing in the present 'dumbing down' of adult television fare. But children's television flourished in Britain in the sixties, partly as a result of the increased exchange of programmes with France and the USA as media frontiers began to dissolve.

By 1960, 75 per cent of British families had television sets; at the same time 47.2 million television sets were operating in American homes (covering about a third of the population). Colour television was just becoming available, following the invention of the Secam system in France, but it was a still luxury item, even in the USA; only 5 per cent of American homes received television in colour by 1961.[1]

Owen Reed, head of the BBC's Children's Department between 1956 and 1964, realized that there had to be swift and revolutionary changes in their children's output if ITV were not to decimate their ratings, so he abruptly abandoned the prevailing rather supercilious stress on 'aesthetic excellence' and directed his energies towards offering 'entertainment'. Witnessing this volte-face was like watching a Victorian lady lurching into a gin palace, but Reed and his team gritted their teeth and pursued the new goal of 'compulsiveness'. At a BBC meeting held on 22 November 1960, Reed laid out his new plan of action for children's television:

> Since competition has had to be urgently reckoned with, compulsiveness – the art of being compulsive – has become one of the standards of good television; that is to say, whether a programme is good or bad is decided not only on whether it is a good or bad programme for children but whether it is a useful thing for keeping children with you, which is a different thing.[2]

While this statement exhibited a certain dash, a declaration of innovativeness proudly proclaimed, Reed himself was deeply ambivalent about both popularity in general and American fare in particular. ITV's American successes filled him with faint nausea. 'I would not touch *Popeye* if it was offered to me on a plate,' he announced at one meeting. On another occasion he declared that *Huckleberry Hound*, a US Hanna-Barbera creation gaining huge popularity on commercial television, 'was agony to watch . . . with its emphasis on violence'.

It is almost impossible to recall how vehemently anti-American the British were at this time, in a period that pre-dated mass immigration from Africa, India and Pakistan in the late sixties; Britain was still a 'tight little island' nursing bittersweet memories of the Second World War while it watched the Empire crumbling piece by piece. When Lew Grade hired Ed Roth from Boston as Deputy Managing Director of ATV in October 1962, there was a media outcry. Grade responded in disgust: 'I wouldn't care if he were Chinese. He's the best man for the job.'[3]

Despite these deep feelings of xenophobia, Britain's Commonwealth brethren were generally acceptable. Even the most bigoted of BBC executives could smile on Canadian artistic creations, for example. This was one of the reasons that *Tales of the Riverbank*, a series made in Toronto in black and white by Dave Ellison, Ray Billings and Paul Sutherland, was admitted to the generally homegrown company of the BBC's afternoon children's television in 1960. The series featured live animals in original stories – a hamster, a white rat and that very North American native, the skunk. The animals were given voices, but they were still presented as wild creatures. When the creators first filmed *Tales of the Riverbank* in Toronto in 1958, it was 25 degrees below zero and one of the makers succumbed to double pneumonia. There was nothing particularly unique about the animals: they came from ordinary pet shops. In fact, the series had the effect of raising the sale of pet-shop hamsters threefold in Canada shortly after its launch.

This was one of the first series to become a global smash hit, winning a hundred television awards over the years, the first from Moscow in 1960. The quaint charm of 'Hammy' and his riverbank chums was further enhanced by using the voice of Johnny Morris in the British version (Morris later graduated to being the star presenter of *Animal Magic* in the sixties).

Ellison moved from Canada to the Isle of Wight in 1972 and made twenty-five half-hours in colour, giving the show an indigenous British flavour. The title of the series was changed to *Hammy the Hamster* in the seventies, and it moved to Granada Television soon afterwards because the BBC introduced a new policy of banning human voices for animals.

Rapid policy changes characterized the BBC under Reed's rule. It was an altogether edgy reign, fraught with indecision, for Reed, despite his talk of compulsiveness, was at heart a deeply dispirited man. The handsomely made classic children's dramas were not pulling in the young audiences. The redoubtable Dorothea Brooking, for example, maker of the original BBC gem *The Railway Children*, was moved sideways into producing the educational-cum-entertainment magazine show *Play School*, in the hope of increasing children's viewing figures. *Play School* ran and ran, being transmitted four days each week initially, five days weekly later on.

Twenty years after his retirement Owen Reed spoke to John Lane of the BBC Oral History Project in 1977:

> What was very difficult to argue against was unfavourable comparisons with the rival programme at the same time, and there appeared on the Wednesday morning conference table in an awful sort of atmosphere of doom what were done as the (competitive) graphs . . . And if at any point in time the programme at that moment showed up unfavourably one was judged unfavourably almost automatically with a sort of awful, neurotic, round-the-table gasp of breath . . . It was figures, figures, figures all the way. And because figures tended to be weaker on the children's side, because of our wretched lack of money and our lack of film and maybe our lack of ability for all I know, there was a wave of what I can only describe as paedophobia, a sort of horror of anything labelled with the name of children.[4]

One glimmer of light shone into Owen's gloom. Even though it was competition, he liked *Robin Hood*. Clutching desperately to this one positive fact, he decided that a certain adventurousness, a romping in sylvan woods, could be both refined and appealing and, better still, raise viewing figures. It was on this timorous supposition that the long-time jewel in the Corporation's crown, *Blue Peter*, was born more than forty years ago.

According to one study, Reed saw *Blue Peter*, transmitted at its fullest and best in 1962 during his reign, as a kind of 'action adventure', incorporating the filming of exotic locations that would best convey a Robin Hood-like flavour of outdoor trekking and action-packed shoots.[5] This was skewed thinking. *Blue Peter* was worthy, and it grew immensely popular as it expanded its caring, club-like activities, but initially it could not compete with the excitement and professionalism of *Robin Hood*. Such home-grown attempts to emulate the gloss and pace of a polished Hollywood product only served to hasten the end of his rule. Reed was a sad man wrestling with his own principles; at heart he loathed trying to emulate this Californian sheen and ruefully recalled the early days of the BBC's 'relaxed and civilized thinking'.

When Owen Reed decided to amplify *Blue Peter* to compete with adventure series such as *Robin Hood*, he was building on a magazine show that had already made a strong start. It was the brainchild of John Hunter Blair and was first transmitted on 16 October 1958, introduced by the late Christopher Trace, then a 25-year-old former army officer and actor, and Leila Williams, a 21-year-old blonde and former Miss Great Britain of 1957. Williams was very pretty with shapely, nyloned legs. The show was only fifteen minutes long and was transmitted once a week. It consisted of Christopher Trace demonstrating model railway layouts and Leila showing dolls. The show was sparse and cheap to produce, featuring none of the campaigns and paraphernalia of the later hit show – no pets, no badges, no lifeboats. Two items leavened the thin mixture: Tony Hart told and drew stories about Packi, the baby elephant (later a real baby elephant appeared, the one that famously relieved itself on the set); and the familiar theme song 'Barnacle Bill' remained its signature tune.

Owen decided to give the show a boost. He hired Biddy Baxter, to take charge in 1962, first becoming its producer and then its editor three years later. The programme appeared every Monday and Thursday for ten months of the year, usually filmed in Studio One at Television Centre, at the time the largest production studio in Europe (which was necessary for the troupe of five hundred Girl Guides who appeared in one show, for example). Biddy knew her child audience – eight- to ten-year-olds – and cherished them (no paedophobia here!). As she later recalled:

> Children are the most selective audience. If they are bored they either switch off or switch over . . . You don't want to talk down to them, but when you think of the mixed abilities of the audience you must do a lot of items on two levels. The little ones will appreciate the visuals and the older ones will take in the information.
>
> Seventy-five per cent of the ideas for the show are suggested by the children themselves. For their trouble, they are awarded a *Blue Peter* badge. Once this happens, their names join the other hundreds of thousands on a card-index system in the show's Special Correspondence Unit.
>
> Being a live programme we can be topical. We have shown such horrendous situations as starving children in Biafra, but it would be quite wrong to show this if you didn't tell the audience you could do something to help. The show is far more than just showing children how to make toys from household scrap.[6]

With its appealing presenters Valerie Singleton (and her famously figure-hugging belted mackintosh), zany John Noakes and the handsome straight man Peter Purves, the show hit on a winning streak. It had miraculously tapped into that previously undiscovered pool of compassion for others that children possess, and it also recognized that the young have a potent wish to be part of a larger, helping group – to be joiners, in fact (hence the power of the *Blue Peter* badge).

Most grown-up viewers of the early programmes recall 'doing something with egg-boxes and toilet rolls'. That reputation endures, especially as the show is still going strong and retains this do-it-your-self formula for creating both artistic and utilitarian objects. Recently

Lynn Barber of the *Observer* described the abstract sculptor Sadie Coles, a controversial Tate exhibitor who makes intriguing conceptual forms out of beer cans and cigarette butts among other pieces of rubbish, as creating forms with 'an assembly of *Blue Peter* household materials'.[7] She didn't have to explain what she meant.

Blue Peter was an original programme with its own distinctive characteristics, and it was as British as Her Majesty the Queen. All the same, it had taken a leaf or two from an American pre-school series, *Romper Room*, especially the stress on persuading the young audience to 'be good' or at least altruistic. *Romper Room* was being transmitted from Anglia Television in the early sixties, when *Blue Peter* was a vital ratings-raiser for the BBC, as Reed and his colleagues were acutely aware. Former Granada Television Chairman Denis Forman recalls in his memoirs, *Persona Granada*:

> Throughout my time with Granada there was a state of cold war between the ITV companies and the BBC. Each side never ceased to plot and scheme ways of outsmarting the other . . . I did my best to seek ways of working with the BBC when it was obvious that this would result in a better deal for the viewer, as with the Olympic Games, which we both had the right to cover. In this I was greatly assisted by three people – Huw Wheldon, David Attenborough and Paul Fox – all three great broadcasters and all prepared to put the viewers' interest ahead of any feelings of petty rivalry, which were even more rife within the BBC than in ITV.[8]

So perhaps there was a little blood on the kindergarten floors of *Romper Room* when Anglia Television began to screen it. It had a simple format for its audience of pre-schoolers, created by Chicagoan Nancy Claster, the show's formidable presenter 'Miss Nancy', who had a neat roll of brunette hair and a tendency to beseech her studio audience and outside viewers to 'be good', ending her programme by waving into a mirror frame.

Romper Room originated in Baltimore, Maryland, in 1953. In the beginning, different kindergarten teachers appeared on their own local television stations after a week's training with Nancy Claster and her husband Bart at the Romper Room School. They recited poetry, taught rhymes and instructed their small group of studio children (usually about seven boys and girls) in simple sums and the acquisition of gentle good manners). The shows were syndicated across the USA and by the sixties were being transmitted in many countries – Canada, Australia, New Zealand, Japan and Malaysia. Anglia Television took the Canadian version, presumably preferring its toned-down variety of North Americanism.

English-speaking Canada was particularly keen to give the show a homegrown flavour, true to its fear of being assimilated by its powerful neighbour: 'To make the show more Canadian, on-location shooting is undertaken in various parts of Canada, reflecting Canada's geography, history and culture. Canadian books are used to introduce parents and children to Canadian writers, illustrators and publishers.'[9] None the less, Canada was open to the best of American television for children and did not always insist on giving the shows a Canadian complexion. The famous American programme maker Fred Rogers started his children's series *Mr Rogers' Neighborhood* in Canada, and it was transmitted unadapted from there in 1968. It was a simple mix of fact and fantasy, using Rogers's songs and two hand puppets and giving out strong, encouraging messages to the under-sixes about how to feel good about themselves. Though initially only fifteen minutes long, it was an immediate hit. A year later Rogers took *Neighborhood* to the USA, amplifying the programme to a thirty-minute slot. It played nationwide via local public service stations. My niece Virginia Biggs watched it regularly with her two little girls when in Iowa in 1969. She recalls: 'The programme was broadcast by Pittsburgh's public service station WQED-Television. The children would sing along to "It's a Beautiful Day in the Neighborhood" and watch Mr Rogers provide the voice and motion to a set of hand puppets. He was always dressed in a comfortable cardigan sweater and spoke to the camera as if you were his own private guest. He was soft-spoken and very mild-mannered. Rogers's place was quiet and intimate. Hanna-Barbera's creations seemed frenetic by comparison!'

Monica Sims, head of Children's Programmes at the BBC from 1967 to 1978, says of *Mr Rogers' Neighborhood*: 'I admired the programme enormously and we showed several episodes, as I recall. We appreciated its principles of altruism.'

Fred Rogers was an ordained minister and was openly Christian but with a small 'c'. 'The whole idea', he told CNN interviewer Jeff Greenfield on the thirtieth anniversary of his brilliantly successful show, 'is to look at the television camera and present as much love as you possibly could to a child who might feel that he or she needs it.' He wrote his own songs – about two hundred of them – and concentrated on what he believed to be children's interests, fears, sibling jealousies, sexual curiosity and feelings of inadequacy. When his pet goldfish died he used the occasion to talk about love and loss. 'He's a singing psychologist for children!' one women's magazine writer trilled to her readers.

His 'All You Need Is Love' approach only slipped once. In December 1998 he filed a lawsuit in the Pittsburgh federal court over a Texas novelty store chain's sale of T-shirts showing his photo with a superimposed handgun and the slogan 'Welcome to My Hood' over it. He demanded that the T-shirts be destroyed. For a man who had always eschewed merchandising of any kind during the thirty years of his show, this piece of commercial exploitation seemed especially cruel and incongruous. His fans loved him even more for turning tough when circumstances demanded it.

With shows such as *Blue Peter, Romper Room* and *Mr Rogers' Neigh-*

borhood all preaching the virtues of behaving well and loving your neighbour, it was difficult not to feel that Anglo-American youth was being fed an over-rich diet of rectitude. But in 1965 help was at hand in the form of the animated series from France, *The Magic Roundabout* (*Le Manège Enchanté*) by Serge Danot. The French version had undoubted charm. Incidentally, the now famous dog, Dougal, who looked like a silky toothbrush with a parting down the middle of his back, was called Pollux in the French version and spoke with a heavy English accent – an immediate rib-tickler, apparently, for French audiences young and old.

Eric Thompson, the actress Emma's late father, was given the job of writing an entirely new script for the English version, and he did it wonderfully, for his scripts were always airy and light-hearted yet knowing. For the first time parents tuned into a programme with their children, enjoying the satirical references to sixties' counterculture. Dylan was a perpetually 'stoned' guitar-strumming rabbit busy growing mushrooms in his vegetable patch, his name doubtless a tribute to the musical idol, who was of course never directly mentioned. Dougal subsisted on a supply of sugar (for his acid trips?), and Brian the snail inched out of his shell-capped torpor on occasion with an accelerating handful of what one presumed were amphetamines. Not that the show's English adapters ever admitted to including such jokes, and much of the programme was in any case straightforward pre-school fare. But when the mustachioed iron coil Zebedee said 'Time for bed' at the end, children tended to take notice, for Zebedee was an assertive, even intimidating little character.

I interviewed Eric Thompson at the BBC's White City cafeteria for *Nova* magazine in the late sixties, and while he was charming he was giving nothing away. How did he get his ideas, I asked. 'Oh, they just come to me before I drop off to sleep at night,' he told me amiably and inscrutably. My notebook was bare as I parted from him, enthralled by his charm. Yet reruns of the programme are well worth watching even today, for this was a remarkably acute and sophisticated show that worked on two levels, for adults and children alike. When Dougal gets cross he says, 'I'll tell NATO', and later suggests that if people want you to keep off the grass, 'Vote Conservative'. When Dylan wakes up one morning to see how his garden has grown, he says, 'Wow, look what's sprung up overnight!' (mushrooms), to which Zebedee retorts in the corny vein loved by children, 'There won't be much room for anything else.' Geddit?

Something about the gentleness of *Romper Room* and its soothing presenter Miss Nancy convinced the BBC children's television programme-makers that this was the right attitude to strike with their own under-fives. Joy Whitby was brought in to set up the daily programme *Play School* in 1964; Anna Home and Dorothea Brooking, among others, formed the nucleus of producers to create the show, which also incorporated the story-telling feature *Jackanory*. Later, in 1967, a spin-off programme, *Play Away*, was added on Saturdays; again parents watched it avidly with their children (and with stars such as Kenneth Williams and Brian Cant this was not surprising).

The conviction was growing that it was not necessary to choose between entertainment and learning; one blended into the other, and as long as *Play School* did not actively attempt to teach the three Rs, which BBC Schools programmes were set up to do, there would be no problem. Thus some of the far-reaching discoveries of the decade about how children play and learn, associated with the names of Benjamin Bloom, Jerome Bruner and Basil Bernstein – the 'three Bs' – had filtered into the BBC's executive suites. It may seem a truism today, but in the sixties the discovery that children did not differentiate between learning and play was revolutionary. The 'three Bs' also maintained – and backed up this assertion with their research – that children absorb more than half of their lifetime's learning in the first five years of their lives. It was time, therefore, to stop making programmes in which marionettes came squeaking out of garden jars. On with more challenging fare.

Play School was an engaging pot-pourri of art, original music, stories, lessons on making things, interactions with pets, information about clocks and other household ornaments, and so on. However, its actual birth was so overpoweringly ironic that it almost drowned in its own baptismal font.

The BBC executives decided to launch their new BBC 2 channel on 21 April 1964. The atmosphere at the opening was electric. Celebrities sat at candlelit tables in the London reception hall waiting to give interviews about their hopes for the new channel. The air was full of promise, as glossy as the sheen on an Oscar nominee's forehead on Hollywood presentation night. Then – zap – the electricity failed, and the new television channel was plunged into darkness. And it did not kick into action until 11 a.m. the next morning, when the channel opened with the door and window of . . . *Play School*.

Play School may not have warranted such a breathless beginning, with the nation's eyes turned mockingly upon it, but it *was* a groundbreaking show for pre-schoolers all the same. It did not have a huge budget – the redoubtable Dorothea Brooking still had to create props out of orange crates and such – but it had an inimitable brio and buzz.

Jonathan Cohen, its accompanying pianist and musical director, a smiling, cheerful man of six foot three inches, told me what the show was like when he first arrived in the studio at the age of twenty-one in 1967: 'We were flying by the seat of our pants most of the time. There were no rules to begin with, and as we had a small budget the producers had to write the scripts. There was a huge chasm between ourselves and top management. I can't even remember who the Director-General was at the time.' (In fact it was Hugh Carleton Greene, credited with having an enormously liberalizing effect during his rule from 1960 to 1966.)

Jonathan modestly attributes his huge success on *Play School* to his possession of a celesta for his upright piano. A celesta is a keyboard instrument consisting of a set of graduated steel plates struck with hammers that makes a piano sound 'tinkly', he explained. 'You'd be amazed how the animals responded to the celesta. The parakeet would start to bob his bottom around on his perch, the goldfishes, Bit and Bot, began butting their heads on the bottom of the fishbowl, and even the rabbit got friskier.'

The free atmosphere was infectious both to man and to beast, apparently. Jonathan did the accompaniments for *Jackanory*, in which a personality, usually a West End star, read a story to the children. Bernard Cribbins, Kenneth Williams and Celia Johnson were some of the best-known readers. 'Kenneth Williams was the most camp of them all, unsurprisingly,' recalled Jonathan. 'He read *The Land of Green Ginger* and wore a turban. When he said goodbye at the end, he really strung out the goodbyeeeeee and his eyes bulged and he seemed to go a bit wild. I thought the children would be terrified, but they loved him.'

There were no rules for *Play School* or *Play Away* at first, but they evolved over the years. 'The cardinal rule was that we were never to say, "Go ask your parent to help you", because we knew we would be addressing foster-children and orphans, too. So on the "make" items we'd always say, "Ask a grown-up to help." Referring to a parent was strictly taboo.' There was also a tacit assumption that parents might be absent because an au pair or nanny was in charge of the child. Thus the BBC's children's programmes were undoubtedly scintillating, but many critics felt they were too middle class. Jonathan Cohen says that everyone on *Play School* had a cut-glass educated accent and used 'received English pronunciation'. 'When one of the entertainers was pretending to speak in a Cockney accent, you could almost feel him or her breaking a jawbone to sound like a *bona fide* East Ender. "Cockney" came out like "Corkaney".'

Tim Brooking told me that his mother, Dorothea, suffered from the criticism that the BBC's programmes were perceived as too middle class. 'The executives reduced the number of classic serials she made, adaptations from famous children's books such as *The Secret Garden*, because they said they were too middle class. She replied that council tower-block children loved the classics as much as anyone and accused them of reverse snobbery in declaring the opposite. It was a bitter struggle. My mother was an egalitarian. The last thing she wanted to be accused of was elitism.'

Middle class or not, *Play School* was a triumph in the eyes of Monica Sims, the new head of Children's Programmes who took control for eleven years from 1967. She wrote that it offered 'no directive to learn but constant encouragement to play – with games, rhymes, stories, songs, movement, sounds, painting and dressing-up. To find out, make, build, watch, enquire, listen and help. To experiment with water, shapes, textures, movement and sounds. To wonder, think and imagine.'[10]

Reading this, it comes as no surprise that she turned down the offer to buy *Sesame Street* from the Children's Television Workshop in New York in 1969. When I interviewed her for *Nova* at the time of her rejection at the BBC's White City headquarters she showed no trace of regret. Her blue eyes sparkled as she said how much she had loved Jim Henson's Muppets, but she didn't believe that the poverty-stricken children its director, Joan Ganz Cooney, was initially trying to reach and educate in New York City (later it was beamed at all inner-city American pre-school children) had exact counterparts in Britain. She also thought the language differences – 'trash' for 'rubbish', etc. – would prove a barrier to young viewers. If she was taken aback by its subsequent success on ITV and Channel 4 she never admitted it. In her view she had a very good pre-school programme in *Play School*. Why diminish the chance of producing a successful homegrown show by spending money on an inferior foreign product? Cash was not abundant. Spend what you have on what you have in hand, her thinking went.

During the sixties glove puppets became variety star performers and infused short time slots on both ITV and BBC with their peculiar brand of irreverence and mischief. Three of the most popular were Basil Brush, Emu and Lenny the Lion. Basil Brush, a fox, had a manic laugh and a 'Boom Boom' punchline; he was invented by Ivan Owen to use on Associated Rediffusion's *The Three Scampis* in 1962. Emu, an evil, spoon-billed bird worked by Rod Hull, was later immortalized when he attacked Michael Parkinson on the latter's BBC 1 chat show. Few who saw it will forget Emu pecking a giggling, half-terrified and helpless Parkinson to the floor.

Pauline Shaw, who worked at Granada as producer and director, says she found the 'vents', as she calls the ventriloquists, a rather eccentric breed. She says Terry Hall, Lenny the Lion's puppet-master, began speaking in his Lenny voice as soon as he had removed the puppet from his suitcase in her office in Manchester. 'The minute Lenny came into view and was on his hand', she told me, 'Terry would switch into his Lenny voice. This, even if he was conversing with me about such brass-tacks show-business matters as expenses, studio venues or timings. We always thought the vents were a bit odd, a race apart.'

None the less puppets, big and small, whether operated by an eccentric master or not, came into their own in this era. A new technique for use with miniature wooden puppets called 'stop-frame animation' came into popular televisual usage. The puppet (or a Plasticine model) is filmed at the standard speed of twenty-five frames a second; the film is then stopped, the puppet is moved a little, then filmed for another second, and so on. When the sections of film are run together the puppet appears to be moving – walking, turning, climbing.

The new technique was an essential ingredient of *Camberwick Green*. Gordon Murray brought this programme to children's television as part of the BBC's *Watch With Mother* series in 1966. In 1967 there followed *Trumpton* and then *Chigley* in 1969. Brian Cant was the narrator for the series. Trumpton, a village in Trumptonshire, was the picturesque location for all the action. The centrepiece of the village was the clock tower, and the main joke was that it possessed a fire brigade that boasted shiny and stunning equipment but could never find a decent fire to put out; even the smoke from a Guy Fawkes bonfire could produce wild anticipation in the little firemen, no more than two inches tall on their lilypad-like feet.

The only learning aspect imparted to children that I could discern from watching the programme on video was that these little villagers had an array of occupations of which they were inordinately proud: clockmaker, grocer, window-cleaner, butler, farmer, rag-and-bone man, flower-seller, artist, printer, telephone repair man, and so on. I suppose the telling of time could count as part of the *Camberwick Green* curriculum. *Trumpton* would begin with the town clock striking nine o'clock and end with a band playing.

The Trumptonshire characters were very prosaic. They revered their own professions and adhered rigidly to their occupational rules; magic held no sway in this imaginary village (probably somewhere in middle England, Gordon Murray suggested recently in a BBC Radio 4 interview, because it was rather mountainous). The fire brigade had a catchy rallying cry which was chanted before they set off on their usually futile searches for a fire: 'Pugh, Pugh, Barney McGrew, Cuthbert, Dibble and Grub.'

It would be difficult to discover more devoted followers of a children's programme than the now grown-up viewers of the Trumptonshire saga. Recently I met 37-year-old Rosalyn Watson, a needlepoint-maker and Camberwell market stall exhibitor, who said she that remembered almost all the rhymes from the series: 'My family and I had just moved into a south-east London tower block flat, and I was about six when I watched *Trumpton*. I was wild about it. It seemed to me to be just about the most perfect village ever. Maybe it had something to do with my living in a new sixties' council block, but I don't think so. I think it would have appealed to me anyway. And my mother approved of it. She wasn't the kind of mother who let us watch any old rubbish to get us off her hands. She rationed what my sister and I watched. The "Pugh, Pugh" fireman's rhyme was practically our signature tune.'

Gordon Murray is very casual about the famous rhyme. He says he found most of the names in a telephone book. 'It is the rhythm of the verse that counts', he insisted on Radio 4, 'and not the names themselves.' He added wearily, 'People *would* keep saying "Hugh, Pugh". They were twins, you see – Pugh, Pugh.' The Trumptonshire trio has become such a cult series that Murray's occasionally opaque explanations of its conception emerge as from the lips of a biblical prophet (twins with the same name?).

However, the series' undoubted charm has produced some very serious thoughts on its true meaning. One devotee explained to me that the show was reflecting the importance of job demarcation lines: the unions had reached the zenith of their power in Britain in the early and mid-sixties, and Trumptonshire reflected this political fact. Perhaps so: children's television certainly mirrored its times.

But to see the Trumptonshire residents once again on a new video is enough to make one smile. They have heads the size of ping-pong balls, they lack mouths, they walk about as if on magnetic pads, and the men are almost invariably bald with nothing but woolly, crescent-shaped fringes at the back for hair. And they walk haltingly; the stop-frame technique often seem more stop than go. But they work like beavers, recite their rousing jingles and never go on strike.

Even though there were no significant children on the series (except for a supine infant called Baby Honeyman and two children with small roles) child viewers loved it. The producers of Trumptonshire had made a profound discovery in an undoubtedly rather casual way: young viewers do not always have to see other children portrayed in a series to become absorbed by its events.

Children's television-makers do not, in spite of their strong wish to entertain the young, work in isolation from world events. *The Magic Roundabout* allowed its French creators, and later its British adaptors, to luxuriate in fantasy, but this is quite rare. By and large, cataclysmic world happenings do intrude upon the content of children's serials in particular.

In any case, the mood had changed at the BBC with the appointment of Doreen Stephens, head of the Children's Department, a woman who kept a strong hand on the tiller from 1964 to 1967. There were not going to be any 'cosy fairy fantasies', she announced firmly; the 'soft and sentimental' approach of *Watch With Mother*, with its 'denial of experience' and perceived middle-class bias, was out. 'Television', she proclaimed, 'had a duty to enrich and enlarge the child's experience – over-protectionism was at an end.'[11]

Looking back, it seems ironic that such a clarion call for the introduction of 'reality' should result in a plethora of science-fiction programmes peopled with reptilian monsters and surreal machines from outer space. But out in the real world a series of mind-bending space odysseys was fast blurring the boundary between science and science fiction. The USA and the Soviet Union were engaged in a struggle to conquer space – a race which the West looked like losing. What is more, putting a man into space required an intercontinental ballistic missile, and Russia obviously possessed the mightier rockets. Yuri Alekseyevich Gagarin was launched into a single earth orbit on 12 April 1961; the following year the Soviets launched two manned spacecraft in nearly identical orbits one day apart. Sometimes animals, notably a dog called Laika, accompanied the astronauts.

The BBC responded to these momentous world events by reorganizing its departments. It decided that some new children's programmes, serials largely, should be transferred from the Children's Department to Drama. Budgets were slightly increased, and there was some head-hunting for respectable West End stage and cinema actors.

Script-writers and composers were also sought. There was a serious need for a cracking good sci-fi series, both to serve as a dramatic kick-off for the new department and to keep pace with the chilling race occurring in space itself.

It was Sydney Newman, a former Canadian Broadcasting Corporation executive and the originator of a children's serial first transmitted in 1959, *Pathfinders in Space*, who was chosen for the job of producing a new sci-fi serial. His brief was sketchy. 'They told me that they were looking for something to bridge the gap between the after-noon sports programme and *Juke Box Jury*. Some kind of children's drama. And what dropped into my mind was H.G. Wells's time machine. I'm not sure precisely how the idea developed, but what I thought was we could have some characters who would travel back-wards and forwards in time. They would come into contact with either real historical events or else meet things in the future that were feasible. Everything had to be possible – what I didn't want were bug-eyed monsters!'[12] (It has to be said, however, that Newman's protest about not wanting 'bug-eyed monsters' in his new science-fiction serial does not ring quite true when one surveys the remaining tapes of *Dr Who*.[13])

Weaving their way through myriad episodes were deadly robots. The most fearsome, to my mind, were the fur-covered Yeti, created by Mervyn Haisman and Henry Lincoln for 'The Abominable Snowmen' in 1967. In the same year appeared the Macra, created by Robert Bank Stewart – large pullulating crab-like creatures who lived on poisonous gas (unfortunate earthlings were forced to quarry the gas, the Macras' virtual oxygen). Sometimes the monsters would be hapless, fluttery insects like the Menoptera who starred in 'The Web Planet' (1965). These were no less horrible for being weak. With bulbous black eyes and wasp-like stripes encircling their narrow middles, they had anten-nae resembling elongated elk antlers, and it was obvious that they wanted nothing so much as to go home to some unspeakable nest (so did the under-tens who watched them, no doubt).

Dr Who was a brilliant creation. The monster-makers were referred to in television studio language as 'activators': after all, these creatures all *moved*, creeping, slithering, rolling, stumping away, sometimes oozing elemental juices on their way. Sydney Newman has said he owed his idea to his impassioned early reading, the H.G. Wells and Jules Verne adventure fiction fare of his youth, *The Time Machine* and *Twenty Thousand Leagues Under the Sea*. Certainly his idea of recreating a Wellsian 'Time Machine' was an inspired one. He called it the 'Tardis', and this structure like a police box, small on the outside but cavernous on the inside, was a master-stroke: it could perform magic for the Doctor and his young companions, zooming them around the galaxy and through time, yet it had an everyday look about it when stationary on planet earth, safe and familiar in appearance. *Dr Who*'s impact often rested on this juxtaposition of the mundane and the extraordinary.

Recently I watched a rerun of a 1970 episode starring the late Jon Pertwee, entitled 'Dr Who and the Silurians', and I experienced the same frisson of terror that must have moved many a young viewer some thirty years ago. The location was earth in this episode, but there is little in its familiarity to comfort one. Ron Grainer's arresting electronic theme tune, shocking in itself, opened the episode as always, ominous and unforgettable at the same time. Dr Who is languishing in a military intelligence sick bay while the Silurians, highly intelligent, man-like reptiles who possess a third eye through which they can focus powerful destructive forces, plot to take over the UNIT, an MI5-like establishment.

Dr Who in this incarnation usually remains rather debonair, no matter how tight a spot he is in. He rarely snaps at anyone to relieve the pressure, although the first Dr Who, William Hartnell, used to scold his teenage granddaughter Susan with tiresome regularity.[14] She was a drably dressed, dutiful mathematics whizz-kid, very different from the attractive mini-skirted female assistants who succeeded her, as the their wardrobes adapted to the new 'swinging' styles of the decade.

The Doctor is an edgy, bright, occasionally snappy idealist. He always knows who is plotting to get him, but he rarely lets his enemies alarm him. Typical of this Noel Coward-like self-possession is his remark to Brigadier Lethbridge Stewart in the Silurian episode. 'Your house is very hot,' he comments jauntily, 'like the reptile house in the zoo.' The Brigadier gets the message, which is a reference to the reptilian nature of the Silurians, and mumbles something about his thermostat being faulty.

At the climax of the episode you see a white-faced robotic Silurian marching towards an innocent farmer and his wife. The raw-boned farmer's wife potters around her kitchen; her husband, a ruddy-faced yeoman, is as innocent-appearing as his animals . . . yet the pair face imminent annihilation at the hands of the featureless robot. There is a dream-like sense of immobilization in the air. Of such inevitability is terror made. Newman made no secret of his debt to James Whaley's *Frankenstein* (1931), and one recalls the monster (Boris Karloff) advancing towards an oblivious little girl playing on a towpath by a stream. There were many script-writers over the thirty years of this serial, but the original themes and contrasts were retained and the character of Dr Who himself changed only slightly, though the dress style and mannerisms of the eight Doctors varied.[15]

A revolutionary twist in the early plot lines of *Dr Who* allowed for the succession of further Doctors ('Time Lords') after William Hartnell. The secret was the phenomenon of regeneration that allowed Dr Who to pass on and to transmogrify himself into a new (and usually younger) doctor. Regeneration was the brainchild of sixties' producer Innes Lloyd and his script editor Gerry Davis. The first regeneration scene was filmed by showing Hartnell's face glowing, then being lost in a blaze of light and finally merging into the quizzical face of his younger successor,

Patrick Troughton. 'The Time Lord is dead! Long live the Time Lord!' Long live the famous science-fiction classic, too! It entertained and delighted viewers from 1963 to 1996, with spin-off films interspersed, and surviving episodes are currently being rerun on television.

Children may have been frightened by aspects of the serial – the ooze, the special effects and the scary make-up – but they loved it all the same. Not everyone was pleased at its phenomenal success, however: predictably, Mary Whitehouse complained about an episode entitled 'The Tomb of the Cybermen', transmitted in 1965; and her angry query about the suitability of the programme for children was discussed in the House of Commons in the late seventies.

Terry Nation's brilliant invention the Daleks capped the serial's early success. These squat metallic creatures with their roller-wheels, metallic casings and electronic monosyllabic speech thrilled young viewers, though they could be unquestionably nasty at times with a Nazi-like ruthlessness about them.

Charlotte Metcalf, now forty-four, a distinguished freelance television documentary-maker, recalls her own excited terror at the programmes. In 1966 she was a dedicated eight-year-old 'behind-the-sofa viewer' (a phrase that has found its way into the vocabulary of children's television analysts and psychiatrists). She told me : 'Of course the Daleks were scary, but because they could talk they sometimes verged on the human, and I started to feel almost affectionate towards them. This feeling was exacerbated one Christmas when my younger brother was given a red-and-white Dalek suit. After that, it was very difficult to take them seriously, and they were demystified for ever. Far more terrifying was the killer foam, which I think was something to do with the Cybermen. Seaweed-like gunk in a sickening froth would slither out of air shafts and ventilators and strangle or suffocate its victim. Before it attacked, steam would slowly start to seep out of the ventilator, followed by the first black tentacle. It was a cross between a squid and a snake writhing around in poisonous foam. It was the stuff of nightmares – formless, mute, deadly and utterly alien as it slid down the walls towards its hapless victim.'

Charlotte Metcalf's comment about her seven-year-old brother's Dalek suit speaks volumes about *Dr Who*, as one of the reasons for its success lay in such spin-off merchandising and the Dalek phenomenon. As a history of the series puts it: 'The overwhelming success of *Dr Who* in the sixties can arguably be traced back to the seven-part Terry Nation scripted story 'The Daleks', which added two new words to the vocabulary of schoolchildren everywhere: "Dalek" and "Exterminate".'[16] For the first time the BBC became seriously commercial and decided to merchandise the Daleks (inspired by all the young fans who wrote in pleading for them to continue: rumours were rife at the time about 'axeing' the silvery villains). The BBC created a licensing department and hired a character-licensing company called William Tucknell Associates. The director, William Tucknell, managed to have a television tie-in with eighty-five different toy and clothes manufacturers by 1965.

While *Dr Who* captivated young British audiences, a not dissimilar series based on intergalactic adventures and misadventures made the ratings soar in the USA. This was Irwin Allen's show *Lost in Space*, which premièred on Columbia Broadcasting System (CBS) in 1965, running for a total of three years, the first season in black and white, the second and third in colour. It was loosely based on J.R. Wyss's *The Swiss Family Robinson*, a tale of a family shipwrecked on a desert island; like the book, the serial relied on the cohesiveness of a plucky, intelligent family tipped into lonely and dangerous exile – in their case, space itself. Professor Robinson and his doughty wife Maureen had three brave, uncomplaining children, two daughters and a son.

Analysts of the programme's popularity with child viewers suggest that they loved the series because children were presented as self-reliant and impeccably behaved, with little need for parental control. One *Lost in Space* chronicler, Mark Phillips, wrote: 'Previously, children were confined to a mundane adult world where they grappled with dating dilemmas, bedtime curfews and peer pressures. Now they were heroes.'[17]

Lost in Space also embodied typical sixties' themes such as the space race, spying and treachery. In fact its link with current events was more than thematic: NASA once used this prime-time show to draw public attention to its own new ventures. The storyline concerned the launch of Jupiter 2 in 1997 (then the distant future, of course) and the Robinson family's landing there. NASA scientists blew down Allen's neck with technical advice, until eventually he barked back: 'Don't concern me with logic!'

Like *Dr Who*, *Lost in Space* peopled the heavens with monsters. While the *Dr Who* creations tended to leave ooze behind them as they moved, like garden slugs, their American counterparts had a penchant for human flesh. For the two episodes of 'The Space Croppers' in 1966, for example, starring the Academy Award-winning actress Mercedes McCambridge, Dr Zachary Smith (the evil Robinson stowaway played by actor Jonathan Harris) romances her hillbilly matriarch character, unaware that she and her clan are growing a crop of plants that feed on human flesh. Dr Smith was the popular joker in the pack of *Lost in Space*. He was camp, and spoke with a rather prissy British accent (still synonymous in the USA with dangerous hanky-panky in that era). He was given to savage acts of attempted sabotage, the most heinous of which was to take a luxurious shower with Professor Robinson's scarce supply of drinking water. Dr Smith catchphrases peppered the language of young America ('Never fear, Smith is here' was one of them). Two rather frothy episodes of a 1968 production called 'The Great Vegetable Rebellion' had the good doctor carelessly plucking a flower from the patch of a giant talking carrot. The carrot threatens the hapless Robinson parents (played by Guy Williams and June Lockhart) with instant death as punishment. But perhaps this was too 'far out': the series ended soon afterwards.

Special effects were rudimentary in 1965, and *Lost in Space* was on a tight budget for an adventure-packed programme. So some of the more stirring episodes had to be produced on a shoestring: tidal waves were produced by sloshing water from a tank over the family hardware, and the monsters had to make do with tacky, unwieldy costumes. In one scene the monster, in real life a bit-part ex-footballer called Lamar Lundy, was clad in bark. He was directed to claw at Robinson as the latter zoomed around in outer space. In reality the professor in this sequence was a six-inch doll suspended by wires who buzzed around the villain. Lundy swiped away at the doll but the perspiration in his eyes behind his tight-fitting mask blinded him so that he kept missing him. Production assistants shouted at him insistently: 'He's right in front of you, Lundy, for God's sakes!' After dozens of sweaty, unsuccessful feints, Lundy trapped the doll in his fist. Then he tore off his mask and his bark costume and ripped the doll to pieces, muttering: 'There, you little bastard!'

During the same period, also in the USA, another innovative science-fiction serial was born: the late Gene Roddenberry's *Star Trek*, an intergalactic saga demanding imaginative special effects (on a fixed budget again!). Desilu, the Hollywood company owned by husband and wife team Lucille Ball and Desi Arnaz, was its budget-oriented backer, and the programme was transmitted from 1965 to 1968 (though film spin-offs and television reruns continue to this day). The first pilot episode was 'The Cage', starring Jeffrey Hunter.

This is the tale of a single spaceship, the USS *Enterprise,* manned by Captain Robert T. April, navigator José 'Joe' Tyler, Mr Spock (he of the pointy ears and satanic look, immortalized by actor Leonard Nimoy – the only character who was an alien, a Vulcan) and 'Number One', an icy, efficient woman who acted as the ship's Executive Officer. In his initial format Roddenberry envisaged the spaceship touching base on the desired planet in the year 1995. It was to be, in his own words, a sort of 'Wagon Train to the Stars'; the familiar and consistent locale was the cruiser-sized spaceship which gave the series a feeling of unity. Unlike some of its sister sci-fi shows, *Star Trek* treated violence with kid gloves (though it could have its chilling moments). With its lasers, desert wastelands, hyper-blue skies and heroes generally dressed in reds and blacks and primary colours, these sixties' sci-fi creations had a strong Pop Art flavour.

As with all television serials – and soaps, too – characters are moved around, altered or removed altogether, largely depending on the ratings (Number One, for instance, was dropped early on in the series, judged by Roddenberry to be a ratings loser). It was the handsome, Elvis-sideburned Captain Kirk (played by actor William Shatner) who turned out to be the leading audience booster, with Leonard Nimoy and his glistening lips following not far behind. They were good role-models for boy viewers: both possessed courteous manners, and the demonic Spock was actually quite controlled. The emphasis was on being wary of enemies and sharply defensive.

There was very little in the programmes that could have upset conservative sensibilities. Racists might not have welcomed the interracial romance on board ship, however. African-American actress Nichelle Nichols, called Lieutenant Uhura in her role as Communications Officer, is filmed kissing Captain Kirk.

The special effects men were, as usual, the unsung heroes of the production team. They had to have more imagination than cash, running as they did on meagre budgets. In *Star Trek* it was John Dwyer, a gigantic beanpole of a man, who spent days scouring unused Hollywood sets and second-hand furniture shops for props: he needed fireplaces, wall panels, old brass lamps, window units. How, he would ask himself, would he find a chair that looked as if it belonged to planet Orion in the year 2300? He somehow managed to make something out of an old piece of furniture. And Dr McCoy's all-purpose 'sensor' – a radiation control device – was a salt-shaker!

Technological jargon was often a problem; how would the actors wrap their tongues around some of the futuristic gobbledeygook? During one scene in the filming of 'The Trouble with Tribbles', for example, Captain Kirk is called upon to find out how the Tribbles – small furry, rodent-like animals with huge appetites – got into an *Enterprise* storage bin of wheat called a 'quadrotriticale'. Actor William Shatner, standing erect, a dashing, gold-braided military figure, was called upon to deliver this immortal line: 'I want to know who put the Tribbles in the quadrotriticale!'[18]

In the early sixties Roberta Leigh, a colleague of Gerry Anderson who had given him a career start by commissioning *Torchy* and *Twizzle* from him, created a stunning sci-fi series: this was *Space Patrol*, which ran in 1963 and 1964 (though it had had several introductory runs in the early fifties). Leigh was original enough in being the first woman to create such scientific adventures; she was also the composer of its theme tunes (which greatly inspired composer Nick Magnus as a child; see Chapter 7).

Space Patrol consisted of thirty-nine episodes of thirty minutes' duration made by Wonderama Productions. It was set in the year 2100 and concerned the adventures of the United Galactic Organization, a peace-keeping force formed by the natives of Venus, Mars and Earth. The crew of Galasphere 347 was comprised of the Earthling Larry Dart, Martian Husky and Venetian Slim. This sci-fi serial, which has recently been made available again on video, has a marvellous, larky attitude to planetary phenomena – weird gases, magic rocks, carbon dioxide clouds and so on – and was much more tongue-in-cheek than many of its rivals. But it had a rough time competing with Gerry Anderson's *Fireball XL5* and *Stingray*, which came out simultaneously. As Roberta Leigh had originally given Anderson his first big chance in show business, this seemed a bit unfair.

As Gerry Anderson confided on a Channel 4 run-down of the *100 Best Kids' Television Programmes* in August 2001, he really wanted to be Steven Spielberg and 'never wanted to work with puppets'. But fate conspired against him: he was a master puppeteer. Born in suburban London before the outbreak of the Second World War, he was evacuated from Neasden to Northamptonshire and had a chaotic childhood shuttling to and fro from city to country as an evacuee. His early years were also scarred by signs of rural anti-Semitism, something which he found difficult to comprehend since he was not a practising Jew. His wartime life was marred even further by the death in action of his brother Lionel. Significantly, this adored older brother had trained in the RAF at a field called Thunderbird.[19]

Like so many of his associates at the time, Gerry was deeply concerned about the conquest of space and had visited NASA while in the USA, keeping a piece of a rocket on his desk in Buckinghamshire where he worked. While he worried about the fact that the West might be falling behind in the space race, his puppet characters in *Fireball XL5*, *Stingray*, *Captain Scarlet* and *Thunderbirds* were not aggressive or bent on the destruction of the USSR (or whoever might represent them). They were generally engaged in exploration – on land, sea and air. Anderson and his dynamic wife Sylvia were not as restricted financially as so many of their contemporaries: Lew Grade, the cigar-chomping tycoon of the Independent Broadcasting Commission, was backing them. For this reason they were able to go straight into colour with *Stingray* in 1965 and to contemplate healthy American sales soon after production. Though he was as English as Marmite, Gerry Anderson is often thought of as mid-Atlantic as a consequence of this success.

Stingray was an underwater adventure series featuring dangers of the aquatic kind (usually huge, hungry fish, as the title suggests). Its hero, Troy Tempest, was a puppet whose features were based on the tough, square-jawed American actor James Garner, star of *The Rockford Files*. Anderson thought that, as viewers were now familiar with outer space, a series set under the sea was the next logical move. 'I had been fascinated to read about trenches in the ocean that are as deep as mountains are high . . . As these are areas of the Earth that have still hardly been explored, I felt justified in writing some wacky stuff. *Stingray* was another example of my interest in anything that involved exploration,' he told his biographers.[20]

Several episodes into *Stingray*'s production a script-writer noticed that their macho puppet hero, Troy Tempest, had a squint. He complimented the director Alan Patillo on this masculine highlight, but it transpired that the facial flaw was in fact an error on the part of the puppet-maker, and surgery was required. One cast member wondered if the medieval Italian carpenter who had fashioned Pinocchio had not had a similar problem with Pinocchio's nose, inventing the story of the puppet's lies to fit the original blunder.

Anderson revered the ancient art of puppetry and knew a great deal about its Chinese origins, Renaissance Italian innovations and Victorian English heyday at seaside pier Punch and Judy shows. He was one of the first to ally the ancient tradition to modern technology. He coined the term Supermarionation when first making *Stingray*. Basically, this meant that the puppets were held up by electronic strings. The early Supermarionettes were made primarily of wood and leather (the latter used as the hinge of the moving lip). Each marionette was between twenty and twenty-four inches tall and had several heads to give the impression of changing expressions – one called the 'serious face', another the 'smiling face'. The puppets weighed between seven and eight pounds and the wires fashioned to hold them were constructed of tungsten steel, twice the thickness of human hair. (Anderson once told a woman interviewer that he was bald because he had used his own hair to suspend them – the journalist believed him and solemnly repeated this innocent leg-pull!)

As he progressed through his popular puppet serials he became more and more sophisticated (in *Thunderbirds*, launched in 1966, for example, lips were made from soft latex; initially the production team tried condoms but the latex proved too unmalleable). Oculists began

67

to make plastic puppets' eyes to add realism, and later on wooden puppet bodies were replaced by fibreglass.

As soon as the eyes and bodies of the puppets had been made more lifelike Anderson turned his attention to their voices and lip movements. An electronic pulse transmitted to a solenoid placed in the puppet's chest cavity activated the bar that moved the lips in synchronization with the vocals, lending verisimilitude to their speech. Puppet garb helped to hide the tungsten wires, matted a black shade to avoid any telltale wire sparkle on film; the wires were also threaded through the puppets' helmets and caps to hide them. Sadly, while the puppets began to look real, especially when seated, they never looked natural when walking. They had an unmistakable wobble.

In *Captain Scarlet*, another Anderson Supermarionation winner of 1967 and 1968, this difficulty was partially circumvented by using the 'sounds' of movement, hence the famous 'walking down the alley and broken bottle' acoustic effect during the serial's opening credits. A teacher friend approaching forty remembers the goose bumps that rose on his arms when he heard those famous footsteps. Eerie sound effects and dramatic musical scores appear to imprint themselves on a child's memory almost more than visuals.

Captain Scarlet was the first of the Anderson shows to have 'perfectly proportioned' marionettes and also the first to have its own production company, Century 21 Productions. The plot was as wacky as Anderson loved to make them: Captain Scarlet is the leader of Spectrum, a world security force waging a war of nerves against the Mysterons from Mars. It also starred some seductive women as Angel Fighter Pilots, one of them a replica of Ursula Andress. Strong women characters were a Sylvia Anderson addition (she became the voice of Lady Penelope in *Thunderbirds*).

In spite of its undoubted ingenuity, and its enormous value to the Andersons in helping them to perfect their Supermarionation techniques, *Captain Scarlet* began to lose viewers and failed to extend beyond its two-year screening schedule. So the Andersons moved on quickly to another puppet programme, transmitting their new science-fiction serial *Thunderbirds* through Associated Television in 1965.

(It was becoming obvious by now that the BBC's near monopoly of original, homegrown children's television had weakened dramatically, helped in no small measure by the Anderson space puppets. Other commercial companies were developing more of an identity, too, not relying on American imports as heavily as they had done in the fifties. Alongside *Thunderbirds*, ATV screened a programme called *Junior Sportsweek*; Associated Rediffusion had a twice-weekly magazine programme called the *Five o'Clock Club*. Granada Television kick-started into action with *Junior Criss Cross Quiz* and a ground-breaking outside broadcast show presented by Desmond Morris called *Zoo Time*. Apparently, children did not always wish to have their animals anthropomorphized, as in *Muffin the Mule*, but liked to know about their real tastes, care and habits. The fascination for wild animals gave charming Johnny Morris, the presenter of the BBC's *Animal Magic* show, a big boost, too, especially when it starred James the winsome orang-utan.)

Thunderbirds became the jewel in Gerry and Sylvia Anderson's crown, though neither of them had anticipated such accolades and commercial success from it. Gerry concentrated his usual energy on its production, putting twelve expert puppeteers on the job; he also reduced the size of the puppets' heads in the interest of realism and had a dentist in Maidenhead fashion real teeth for them. Their features were made more recognizable, too; this with the help of the faces of real actors (Sean Connery was the facial model for Thunderbird One pilot Scott Tracey, for example).

The gift of surprising originality in puppet characterization emerged strongly with *Thunderbirds*, especially through the two distinctive characters Lady Penelope and her chauffeur Parker. The inspiration for 'Nosey' Parker was a Cockney waiter at the King's Arms pub in Cookham, Berkshire, which the production team frequented. 'He had a warm patter,' Gerry recalls, 'and he kept dropping his h's and putting them back in the wrong places, which intrigued me.'[21]

International Rescue's British agent Lady Penelope Creighton Ward, with her blonde hair with flick-ups, sexy voice and curly eye-lashes, was a plummy English aristocrat, custom-made for American audiences, the Andersons thought. She had a dream country manor house and a luxuriously fitted car. What better way to win top ratings in the USA than by producing popular British stereotypes – toffs and East Enders in close league against their enemies. It had all the Bondian virtues: spies, gimmicks and farcical snobbery. 'Thunder-birds', as they said, 'are go!'

Producing television shows for children wasn't always an easy mat-ter in the sixties, however. Gerry Anderson tangled with the unions on more than one occasion during this decade of union consolidation and supremacy. A union with the jaw-breaking title of the National Asso-ciation of Theatrical Television and Kinematograph Employees insisted he use 'hand artists' for puppet hand motions (such as lifting a cup). It was a laborious and expensive process to have union artisans involved in this way, and Gerry refused. There was grumbling on both sides, but Gerry won.

Besides the dynamic Gerry Anderson, other less flamboyant creators succeeded, too. Two animation geniuses of the time were Peter Firmin and Oliver Postgate, largely retired now and neither as wealthy as they might have been if they had relinquished artistic con-trol over their two most successful joint efforts: *The Clangers* and *Bagpuss*. The latter was voted one of the top ten children's television programmes of the twentieth century several years ago and is rerun regularly on Channel 4.

These two family men, with six children each, originally met at the Central School of Art in London where Firmin lectured. Most of their filming took place in a converted pigsty attached to Firmin's eighteenth-century farmhouse near Canterbury. Firmin's children served as instant audience and critics.

One of Firmin and Postgate's first creations was *Ivor the Engine*, made in 1959 in black and white and aired in 1960 on ITV (Associated Rediffusion). The series revolved around a famous little railway in Wales, the fictitious Merioneth and Llantisilly Rail Traction Company Ltd. A dragon, Idris, lived in Ivor's boiler, sometimes giving him the necessary steam for their progress through the Welsh valleys. The engine driver was Jones the Steam and the stationmaster was Dai Station. Completing this very Welsh scenario was Ivor himself whose fondest wish was to join a Welsh choir. Its popularity with children has remained high, with a long-running colour series being broadcast on the BBC in the seventies and a complete video relaunch in 2001–2.

Trailing Ivor slightly but popular none the less was *Noggin the Nog*, which Firmin and Postgate created shortly after *Ivor*. Noggin was a sweet-natured Viking with a beautiful Eskimo bride. He was constantly being bullied by his evil uncle Nogbad. (Firmin told one reporter that the word Noggin meant a little block of wood and he thought that appropriate for a small, square person.) Postgate added an odd postscript to the feature by confessing that the evil Nogbad was one of his alter egos. As he appears to be an extremely affable man, presumably his inner Nogbad is rather like Churchill's 'black dog', a depressive state which envelops him for brief spells. *Noggin* itself was a rather cheerful animation serial, though it has not lasted as well as the other creations of Smallfilms, Firmin and Postgate's production company.

This low-keyed, polite and modest team were to blast off into stardom like a Cold War rocket soon after this when the BBC asked them for a space-type adventure programme. This became *The Clangers*, which was an extraordinary confection – as if Beatrix Potter had had a wild affair with Salvador Dalí. It was first transmitted on 18 November 1969 and was the BBC's first children's series in colour, all twenty-six episodes of it.

Its screening happened to coincide with an Apollo moon mission, which was an odd juxtaposition since the Clangers had little in common with American astronauts. They were little long-nosed creatures with pink knitted bodies who whistled as they beetled around the moon's surface. Their moon was a cratered blue planet covered in metal lids under which they hid and lived, keeping safe from falling rock bits and other dangerous objects from outer space. A Soup Dragon coexisted with them, providing the Clangers with green soup. Food loomed large in their minds: they loved Glow Honey and blue string pudding. Their high-pitched whistling reached screech pitch when they radioed something called the Iron Chicken who lived in the sky in a spiky nest . . . Strange indeed, but children loved it, especially those of pre-school age.

Bagpuss appeared in 1974. Its hero was a fat, lazy, pink, grey and white cat, owned by Emily, who rested on a cushion in a shopfront window. He came to life only when a group of mice disturbed him by playing their mouse organs (intentional pun). The rest of the storefront cast were Madeleine the doll, Gabriel the banjo-playing toad and Professor Yaffle, a wooden woodpecker bookend.

I was surprised at the simplicity of the story-lines when I watched it during a repeat viewing – only thirteen episodes were made, but it has been shown on the BBC twenty-seven times over the years. Certainly the jowly cheeks of the somnolent cat have an enduring charm. A teacher friend of mine, aged fifty-one, who has a passion for the cat, says: 'Bagpuss is Marmite for the soul.'

Postgate and Firmin never became rich, but they are content. Postgate told a *Daily Telegraph* reporter that he has never regretted not making a fortune through merchandising. 'We didn't have committees, we weren't answerable to a particular school of educational psychology or over-burdened with technology. We just played around with what was around us,' he said.[22]

It is true that the Postgate–Firmin puppets were as far from high technology as they could be. The two men worked surrounded by broken Meccano sets. The Clangers were constructed from an articulated skeleton of wood joined with Meccano pieces and clamp plates. They were stuffed with chopped foam and held together with tight woollen skins. Their feet were made of wood with three holes in them so that they could be pinned down with thumb tacks. Their fingers and the rims of their ears were made of dyed pipe-cleaners. Their planet was constructed out of polystyrene painted blue, and saucepan lids covered their moon hidey-holes.

Television companies today enjoy twitting each other and airing programmes that highlight each other's ludicrous out-takes, and back in the sixties they could be positively incestuous in the way they infiltrated each other. This occurred in a now famous 1972 episode of *Dr Who* in the first episode of 'The Sea Devils'. The imprisoned villain called the Master (Roger Delgado) is seen watching a *Clangers* sequence ('The Rock Collector') and trying to emulate their whistling.[23] His jailer asks him what he is watching. The Master replies: 'It seems to be a rather interesting extraterrestrial life form.' His jailer replies: 'Only puppets, you know.'[24]

3
The Seventies

Healthy Competition, Time-Warps and Reality Viewing

As we have seen, the television fare of the sixties for children was larky, imaginative and frequently puppet-driven. The seventies, in contrast, presented parents and teachers with a far more stringent dose of reality for their young charges. If the sixties offered its young intergalactic fantasies, scary monsters and whistling moon creatures, the seventies' producers performed an about-face. Children would see news programmes and series about working-class children in state secondary schools; even fantastic creatures, when they appeared, often delivered high-flown moral messages about such matters as the deteriorating environment.

Stuart Hood, the BBC's controller of Television Programmes, whose reign stretched from the early to the mid-sixties, had inveighed against the 'middle-class values' of the BBC's programming, but curiously his cavilling did not have any strong effect until after his departure. In 1970–2 the Corporation began to concern itself strongly with the matter of 'cultural deprivation' and class-based differentials in academic achievement. Trainee producers from the Children's Department were sent out to watch programmes in working-class homes and council flats 'in order to get a sense (particularly) of the reactions of working-class audiences'.[1]

Both the BBC and the ITV companies were being nipped at the heels by a new regulatory body chaired by Harry Pilkington and strongly critical of cultural and political laxity in programming. The Pilkington Committee's Report of 1962 had praised the BBC for its cultural diversity but criticized the commercial television companies for being too imitative, accusing them of 'down-market competitiveness'. Stung by this criticism, the ITV companies began to sharpen and streamline their own programmes, paying vastly more attention to children's television. Such outside criticism was salutary for the media as a whole, and it led from a BBC monopoly to a 'healthy duopoly', something the Pilkington Committee had been urging upon them. ITV began to devise clever, anarchic variety shows with top young entertainers. For instance, Lenny Henry starred in *Tiswas* in 1974, an ATV Saturday morning favourite in which much water and gunge was thrown about, thick make-up worn and wisecracks crackled; and there was *Magpie*, a 1972 Thames Television magazine programme, which starred three bright 'twenty-ish' presenters and was a realistic, fast-moving, journalistic show for eight- to eighteen-year-olds with pretty, braless Susan Stranks capturing avid adolescent attention.

Hanna-Barbera cartoons were still a Saturday morning mainstay, with a large diet of *Tom and Jerry* episodes; while some adults considered them violent, most parents and teachers agreed that children would realize Jerry wasn't going to remain for ever squashed under Tom's paw.[2] As one irreligious Granada television presenter assured me: 'At least, watching *Tom and Jerry*, your kids are going to end up believing in the Resurrection.'

Regulatory bodies were stirring in the USA, as well. The Federal Communications Commission (FCC), a somewhat indecisive organization established in 1934 to ensure that radio and, later, television stations were serving the 'public interest', was finding it hard to escape savage criticism from high-powered intellectuals, the most potent of whom was Robert Hutchins, former President of the University of

Chicago. In response, the FCC scolded the US television companies in 1962, saying it would no longer tolerate the 'egregious abuse of public trust . . . and the gap between licensees' promises and actual performance'.[3] As Newton N. Minow, appointed chairman of the FCC in 1961, explains in his book *Abandoned in the Wasteland*[4] – a phrase borrowed from his own powerful comment on what he believed to be the sensation television gave its viewers – the FCC was prevented from the start from having any real regulatory effect by the fact that no one actually knew what 'public service' meant. As he puts it rather equably, considering how difficult his position must have been: 'No one in Congress defined what the public interest clause was supposed to mean in broadcasting.'

Robert Hutchins's eloquent broadside delivered at the time could not have helped: 'We have triumphantly invented, perfected and distributed to the humblest cottage throughout the land one of the greatest technical marvels in history, television, and have used it for what? To bring Coney Island into every home. It is as though movable type had been devoted exclusively since Gutenberg's time to the publication of comic books.'

It was at this time that Peggy Charren, a young New England mother of two, personally buttonholed the FCC chairman, asking why children's television was so execrable. A still active seventy-five, though no longer president of her watchdog group, she told me recently that she could not fathom why this should be when the literature she read to her children was of such high quality. She got little response from the FCC, so she went home to Newton, Massachusetts, and started a powerful parents' organization, Action for Children's Television. She insists that her group 'was never pro-censorship but very definitely pro-quality'.

In 1961 and then again in 1964 President Lyndon B. Johnson convened the Kerner Commission to examine television to see if it induced violence in its viewers. The President confessed to deep unease about the successive assassinations that had recently occurred (the deaths of President Kennedy and Martin Luther King) and also a rash of urban riots. Subsequently, the Commission announced in a Surgeon-General's report 'that violence . . . on television *did* affect behavior adversely'.

The ground-breaking series for children *Sesame Street*, first aired in the USA in November 1969, was a direct result of the Surgeon-General's report and also President Johnson's federal programme, Head Start, aimed at educating disadvantaged children. At the time it was the most expensive children's series ever televised, costing millions. This money came from a variety of sources, public and private: from Head Start, the US Office of Education and such private corporations as the Carnegie and Ford Foundations. *Sesame Street* was designed, the government stated, as a kind of 'Head Start at home'. It was produced by Joan Ganz Cooney of New York's non-profit organization the Children's Television Workshop.

'We're after the poor kids,' Ms Cooney told me when I interviewed her in New York in 1968, 'mainly because we know the lower-class child's prospects can be improved by viewing. We're trying to supply a great deal of information to the disadvantaged child so that he won't go into school with a deficit. We're going to concentrate on the words that he or she will have probably missed, those propositions such as *over, through, in, out*. We'll avoid concrete words. Poor children probably already know them.'

The *Sesame Street* producers met their ambitious objectives magnificently, aided in no small part by the genius of Jim Henson, the show's Muppet maker. Henson, a young man from Mississippi, had created his Muppets for brief time-slots in such fifties' programmes as the Steven Allen, Ed Sullivan and Jack Paar shows. In 1961 he created his own company, Muppets, Inc., coining the name 'Muppet' from the elision of 'marionette' and 'puppet'. He rejected the wooden look of most puppets of the period, finding them devoid of emotional expression. He crafted his puppets from flexible, fabric-covered foam rubber, giving them supple bodies and large, expressive mouths.

By 1961 he had already created his now world-famous frog Kermit, but neither Henson nor Kermit found superstardom until 1969 when, along with Big Bird, Cookie Monster, Bert and Ernie, Elmo and Oscar the Grouch, they featured on *Sesame Street*. Children found the soft puppets beguiling. It did not seem difficult for four- and five-year-olds to ingest complicated information about sentence construction when they came from the reassuringly soft, mobile mouths of Muppets. Joan Ganz Cooney had scored a global hit which, three decades later, is still screened worldwide (London Weekend Television premièred the series in Britain in 1970; presently Channel 4 shows it at 6 a.m., presumably so that pre-schoolers can give their parents an extra hour or so in bed, since it is still very popular).

But to the astonishment of the industry the BBC's Monica Sims turned the programme down. She was very clear in her objections to it, which she outlined in a paper read to the European Broadcasting Union on 14 October 1971. The series, she maintained, attempted to teach by using jingles and repetition – the rhythm of commercial advertising, in fact – and she found this method offensive. Rather than 'giving children the opportunity for a two-way involvement', she stated, 'it offered bite-sized pieces of information, segmented and unrelated to each other, presented at a hectic pace, and detached from real-life situations'. Its fragmented format, she went on, resembled 'a system of cartoons with constant interruptions . . . failing to start from the child's own particular environment and experience'. In consequence, it was 'authoritarian'.

I remember how hard she tried to be polite about the programme during my *Nova* interview with her at White City (see Chapter 2). She had felt it was too American, she said without any apparent rancour. I persevered. Was there *anything* she'd liked about it? (I was still fired by the programme's aims as outlined by Joan Ganz Cooney.) She paused painfully, closing her eyes in concentration. 'Why, yes,' she said slowly, 'I liked Oscar the Grouch.' But not enough, apparently. Sorry, Oscar.

Several television historians have suggested that residual anti-Americanism played its part in the BBC's decision.[5] I feel quite certain that it did. They were public service broadcasters, after all, and proud of their non-commercial, homegrown output. Monica Sims herself had pioneered the entertainment-cum-educational pre-school programme *Play School* and felt this was good enough as a quality educational show.

However, her action caused ructions in the media world, and Chinese whispers about 'overweening pride' floated around the Corporation's corridors. It did not help her cause that the only children's programme mentioned flatteringly in the BBC's fiftieth birthday celebrations in 1972 was *Muffin the Mule*. According to Anna Home, Sims was 'understandably concerned'.[6]

The row over the rejection of *Sesame Street* had at least one useful effect: it galvanized the BBC Children's Department into creating more 'reality' programmes. Plans for a series centring on young working-class adolescents in secondary school (*Grange Hill*) were germinating in the programmers' minds, and *John Craven's Newsround*, a bright magazine show, was given two weekly 5 p.m. time slots. John Craven was an experienced yet casual presenter, dressing informally and not always sitting stiffly at a desk. *Newsround* began in 1972 with the directive that current affairs should be woven into the items, as well as 'topical events, e.g. the Budget, India, Unesco's expeditions, etc.'[7] America had sneezed and Britain had caught a cold. The prissy middle-classness which had aroused Stuart Hood's ire some years before was now fast disappearing.

During the sixties the BBC had already introduced tougher fare to adult viewers, and this new mood was bound to trickle down to the Children's Department eventually. In 1966 Johnny Speight's corrosive character Alf Garnett, played by Warren Mitchell in the comedy series

Till Death Us Do Part, shocked and delighted the nation. Alf Garnett was a foul-tempered, crumpled, vociferous working-class bigot who despised all permissiveness and was baldly racist (like a great many of his fellow-citizens, it was suspected). Audiences delighted in his perversity (he called his wife, played by the actress Dandy Nichols, a 'silly old moo' just as New York feminists were burning their bras). This was comedy *noir*, signifying an almost adolescent bout of nose-thumbing, and probably cathartic. There were also two sensational plays depicting the grittiness of working-class life: Nell Dunn's *Up the Junction* (1963), set in Clapham Junction, south-east London, and focusing on the personal sorrow of abortion; and Jeremy Sandford's *Cathy Come Home* (1966), a wrenching tale of a young mother and her children being shunted from one squalid lodging to another before she loses her children altogether to the Social Services. Bland children's fare such as *Watch With Mother* was not going to survive unscathed in this climate.

Alongside these changes in television subject matter, there was an increasing incentive for programmers to please a burgeoning viewing audience in the seventies. At the start of this decade more than 40 million colour sets were in use throughout the world – about 31 million in the USA, 5 million in Japan, 1.3 million in West Germany, 1 million in Canada and 750,000 in the UK. Television costume drama series were a revelation when viewed in colour, as anyone who saw *The Six Wives of Henry VIII*, starring Keith Michell, and *Elizabeth R*, with Glenda Jackson, will recall. Hitherto the poor cousin of the arts, television was suddenly becoming a star, and audiences worldwide were clamouring for more of the BBC's splendidly acted costume dramas to be beamed into their living-rooms. The Corporation's reputation had reached its apogee. (It was not until the eighties that commercial television would catch up, notably with Granada Television's *The Jewel in the Crown* and *Brideshead Revisited*.)

Then in 1975 another stunning technological advance was

unveiled: Akio Morita, the head of Sony, introduced Betamax, the first portable video cassette recorder, into the USA. Now, not only were viewers being dazzled by colour, they also began to realize that they could capture their favourite features on video for a lifetime. Sony accompanied the launch of their product with a brilliant advertisement: Bela Lugosi as Count Dracula returns to his gloomy flat, switches on his Betamax VCR and enthuses solemnly: 'If you work nights like I do, you miss a lot of great TV programs. But I don't miss them any more, thanks to Sony's Betamax deck, which hooks up to my TV set.'[8]

Everyone was becoming more technologically sophisticated, it seems. It would be hard to imagine Gerry and Sylvia Anderson producing a sci-fi serial that put their former efforts in the shade, scientifically speaking, but they did. *Space 1999* ran from 1975 to 1977 on BBC 2. Sylvia herself oversaw the design of the wardrobes, making them look glamorous and futuristic at the same time. Until then television had been a poor cousin to the wardrobe splendour displayed in Hollywood films, but she went a long way towards changing this for the fictional husband and wife team who starred: Martin Landau (Commander John Koenig) and Barbara Bain (Dr Helena Russell).

The plot of *Space 1999* revolved around the idea that the moon had been blown out of earth's orbit by a nuclear explosion. The serial showed space-suited astronauts walking on the sands of the moon. For this purpose the Andersons evolved an innovative technique: the cameramen shot at high speed – seventy-two frames a second – which was then slowed down for viewing, causing the actors to appear as if they were floating in the planetary mists. The effect was very impressive, but the actors were devilishly hot in their space-suits and could barely tolerate the three-minute sequences of simulated moon walking.

The plot was rich in episodes concerning the moon: its cosmic clouds, splits (it literally broke in two), collisions, energy beams and so on. Some marvellous British stage actors gave the serial style and panache – Billie Whitelaw, Leo McKern and Margaret Leighton, to name just a few. Margaret Leighton, knowing she was dying from cancer, asked if she could sit down during her sequences. As she played the part of a queen, this was easy. Her 'throne' was a cleverly hidden wheelchair. She died only days after the last shoot.

However, the Pilkington Committee had demanded a 'healthy duopoly', which required the commercial companies to rival the quality of the BBC's output. London Weekend Television rose to the challenge with *Catweazle*, a comic drama series in colour aired in 1970 and 1971. It proved to be as original as anything the BBC had made up to that time. Taking a leaf from the BBC's book in borrowing from fiction, LWT based this two-year serial on a book by Richard Carpenter, who also wrote the television script. It was a tale of fantasy and magic starring a rather gormless refugee from a Norman past, Catweazle. The built-in joke was that Catweazle, an eleventh-century magician with a toad called Touchwood as his familiar, could never get his spells and tricks to work. The actor playing him, Geoffrey Bayldon, dramatized his scruffiness and owl-eyed *naïveté* in flamboyant, stagey style, and he became a television screen favourite of the early seventies (schoolchildren would call each other 'Woodlouse!' and other colourful 'Norman' epithets to match Catweazle's insults).

Recently I watched a reissue of a *Catweazle* episode, first shown in January 1971. In *The Heavenly Twins* guest actor Paul Eddington was cast as a bumbling modern-style conjuror, and a precocious, smart-aleck youngster, Cedric, was played by child actor Gary Warren. It is a remarkably slick production for the time, showing Eddington performing his abysmal 'rabbit-from-a-hat' type tricks to a gaggle of fancily dressed children in a beautiful English country garden. Catweazle's rolling eyes and moth-eaten brown monk's tunic were in eye-catching contrast to Eddington's black tie and top hat, and the two accomplished actors made a wonderfully comic duo as they hashed up their magician's routines. Eddington went on to become one of television's most admired comic actors in the *Yes, Minister* and *Yes, Prime Minister* series of the eighties. Quentin Lawrence directed and produced the *Catweazle* series under executive producer Joy Whitby, and the team is to be commended for pulling a rather meandering fantasy into shape and for being clever talent scouts. *Catweazle* charmed the older child and parents, too, rather like the present *Harry Potter* books by J.K. Rowling.[9]

Though ITV was beginning to make a sizeable impact in its race for ratings with the BBC, it still worked to a shorter schedule than the BBC in the afternoon and weekend children's television time slots (around an hour in contrast to the BBC's 105 minutes). It also needed to work on producing more of its own shows, as it still tended to rely on a high proportion of American imports such as *The Flintstones*.

Originally aired by the American Broadcasting Company in the sixties, *The Flintstones* was winning an ever-increasing number of fans, including adults. This jolly family of cave people headed by Fred Flintstone (who carried a club but never used it, as far as I can recall) pioneered a new trend in television-viewing, that of the combined audience. The Flintstone family lived in the fictional Stone Age city of Bedrock. Fred was a typical Neanderthal, working on quarrying stones at the Bedrock Quarry and Gravel Company. His wife, Wilma, bossed him around unmercifully but did have to satisfy his insatiable appetite for pickled dodo eggs, brontoburgers and cactus cola. They had a pretty little daughter, Pebbles, and neighbouring friends, Barney and Betty Rubble. Actors' voices gave the animation a touch of realism, and the jokes were fast-moving. The Flintstone rallying cry, 'Yabba-Dabba-Do', was universally known.

Viewers, both parents and children, enjoyed the prehistoric sight gags involving Stone Age household gadgets such as an elephant trunk vacuum cleaner and foot-powered motor vehicles. The dialogue was reasonably sophisticated, and sometimes Hollywood actors would take part (Ann-Margret's voice resonated in one episode, Tony Curtis's in another). While Hanna-Barbera did not write the cartoon series for adults ('too risky', they said), they appeared to be flirting with them, at any rate. Parents loved the idea of a hen-pecked caveman and the sight of scrawny, nagging Wilma slaving over a hot bronto-burger. While sociologists were mildly astonished by the new phenomenon of combined adult–child viewing, they did not see any harm in it, as the Flintstones were squeaky-clean. This was a far cry from cartoons such as *The Simpsons* and *South Park*, first aired in the nineties, which were created nominally for children but also to enter-tain adults with their sophisticated references and, especially in the case of *South Park*, with *double entendres* and scatological and sexual allusions.

Thames Television took a brave step in the early seventies. It orga-nized a Children's Television Department under the aegis of Lewis Rudd, a dedicated and charismatic head from 1970 to 1972. As Anna Home, BBC's head of Children's Programmmes at the time, writes in her autobiography, the appointment of Rudd and later of Sue Turner (1972–8) at Thames made it one of the most imaginative providers of good entertainment for children in that period.[10] (She also points out that the best way to produce good children's television is to have a department for it and *not* to buy in with monotonous regularity from outside – a truism, perhaps, but one that companies appear to have difficulty taking on board, especially today with the prevailing bud-getary constraints.)

Borrowing a science-fiction format, which owed something to the success of *Dr Who*, Thames devised *The Tomorrow People*, a tale of four intergalactic pre-teen children who are adept at teleporting ('the art of transporting the human body over considerable distances using either psychic powers or as yet undiscovered laws of physics or scien-tific techniques', as one former fan describes it). As with so many of the best programmes, *The Tomorrow People* was adapted from a novel, *The Visitor*, by Roger Price and Julian R. Gregory. The authors describe the somewhat creepy foursome: 'They seem to be just ordinary kids. A bit quieter than most, perhaps. But they are the Tomorrow People, forerunners of a new race, *homo superior*. Gifted with superhuman powers they are Nature's response to man's aggression: a new species, wiser and more peace-loving than *homo sapiens*, and until more of their race evolve they have intergalactic responsibility for the future of Planet Earth.'

Seventies' children's television tended to favour fictional teenage 'gangs' such as *The Tomorrow People*. Parents seemed to be removed from the equation. Another popular show featuring a gang was *Scooby-Doo* – a BBC import – with a well-known signature tune, 'Scooby-Doo, Where Are You?' This was yet another animated cartoon from the pens of Bill Hanna and Joe Barbera and starred a gentle Great Dane with floppy paws and ears and a permanently surprised expression. This is the eponymous Scooby-Doo who directed his parentless gang of four into dangerous scenarios – with ghosts, criminals, smugglers – and who was himself perpetually terrified of all possibilities of danger. The teenage gang, two girls and two boys, wore the popular gear of the time – neck scarves, flared trousers, short, pleated skirts for girls and jagged, scissored haircuts for boys.

While *Scooby-Doo* captured a rather sophisticated young teen audience, other Hanna-Barbera creations, many of them made in the USA in the sixties, were mesmerizing the under-twelves. Hanna-Barbera knew how powerful the subject of food was to children, and several of their cartoon serials were hymns to young foodies. *Yogi Bear*, created in 1959 as part of the *Huckleberry Hound* series, took some years to cross the Atlantic but was a huge hit when it finally landed in the Saturday morning kids' slot. With his stiff white collar, green tie and matching flat cap, Yogi was the happy-go-lucky scourge of Jellystone Park, a simulacrum of the more sober Yellowstone National Park in the western USA. He was reputed to be 'smarter than the average bear', but, like some happy-go-lucky humans who prefer gambling to hard work, his brains were employed almost solely in a search for his greatest passion – stolen food. What Yogi liked best, apart from an occasional shmooze with Cindy Bear of the short-short blue skirt, was a full 'pic-a-nik' basket. He liked to snatch these from under the nose of the dour Park Ranger Smith. His sidekick, Boo-Boo, benign and accommodating, was just happy to be around if a spare crust dropped out of Yogi's purloined baskets.

Yogi's adventures had the same speed of imagery and scene change as its antecedent, *Huckleberry Hound*. There was a technical reason for this: Hanna-Barbera had perfected a system called 'limited animation', in which a character's pose is held for longer and movement is stylized, with only the eyes needing redrawing to suggest changes of expression. This technique requires fewer drawings. In fact, Hanna and Barbera reduced their drawings output by 90 per cent with this technique, according to biographer Michael Mallory.[11] Many aficionados of animation did not approve of this method – it struck them as cheating, cutting creative corners. Hanna-Barbera disagreed, arguing that pleasing viewers was what mattered most.

Luckily, what the duo lost using this technique was more than compensated for in the wide variety of their cartoon creations. Huckleberry Hound was a sleepy-eyed dog dressed in blue with a silly yellow pillbox hat above his droopy ears. He was a patient, sweet-natured canine who took on a vast spectrum of difficult professions from fireman to matador, maintaining his cool throughout, though everlastingly being tormented by more realistically minded dogs who lacked his *savoir-faire*.

In *Wacky Races*, which was first transmitted between 1968 and 1970, Hanna and Barbera allowed themselves to be playful, indulging their delight in crazy nomenclature and also in this case weird cars. Each ten-minute segment centred on a motor-car race which could take place in almost any corner of the globe. The contestants might be seductive blondes driving pink roadsters (such as Penelope Pitstop, who wore a red helmet and black goggles) or big military gentlemen on bristling wartime tanks bearing aggressive names such as Sergeant Blast. The cast of cars included bullet-proof Model Ts manned by tiny gangland crooks and fabulous models such as the chic black low-slung coupé driven by Big and Lil' Gruesome.

One of the group of racing drivers dreamt up by the duo was Dick Dastardly, who went on from cars to race in flying machines (though he never won a race either on the ground or in the sky). This 1970 off-shoot series of *Wacky Races*, called *Stop the Pigeon*, featured the yellow-faced Dick Dastardly in his red cap and yellow goggles, pursuing an oblivious propeller-driven pigeon with a butterfly net. The bird in question, Yankee Doodle Pigeon, was a patriotic American courier who always delivered his vital messages. Dastardly was the apoplectic villain of the piece whom the noble bird always defeats. Children loved the simple plot of the ugly meanie being bested by a cheerful bird. Hanna and Barbera were fascinatingly diverse but not subtle.

The BBC was doing well with imports such as *Scooby-Doo*, but the spirit of competition proved a spur to the production of more novel shows, which proved they were still past-masters in the art of the surreal. The latest 'walk on the wild side' came in the shape of *Mr Benn*, which the BBC first aired in 1971. Mr Benn, taken from the children's stories of David McKee, was a small, rather nondescript man with a bowler hat who lived at 52 Festive Road, London. The original plain 'Mr Suit', he would walk to a costume shop in a dark alley and be welcomed by a shopkeeper wearing a fez. There he changed into a costume – Ali Baba pants and a turban, say – and would go flying on a Persian carpet and have great adventures in the skies. Captivating as the serial was, its plot line was so simple that it is hard to explain its enormous appeal. On Channel 4's round-up in September 2001 of the hundred best television shows of the twentieth century, chosen by audience vote, *Mr Benn* found its way into the top ten.

A French import, *Hector's House*, called *La Maison de Tu Tu* in

France, also made a splash at this time, using simple soft toys and musical instruments. Hector, a sort of beagle in a flat cap and dunga-ree-style trousers, played a tuba to Za Za the cat and Kiki the frog. The Gallic flavour of the names and absurd tuba-playing dog entranced under-fives. They also loved Hector's hymn to himself at the end where he somewhat self-pityingly referred to himself as 'great big sad old Hector' (could there be hints here of an influence of Paul Tripp's wonderful fifties' movie tune accompanying *Tubby the Tuba* in which the disconsolate instrument sings of his own heartbreaking isolation?). Apparently, programme-makers had realized that children can and do empathize with sadness.

The revived appetite for the surreal was fed by *The Wombles*, which was based on a series of books by Elisabeth Beresford, first published by Walker Books in 1970. Beresford got the idea of the Wombles when walking with her two children on Wimbledon Common. They are strange woodland beasts with long snouts and thick prehensile fingers who have a penchant for wearing ill-fitting, thigh-length jackets and unattractive headgear, caps and bowler hats. They are obsessive, to a degree, about keeping Wimbledon Common tidy and thinking up ways of 'making good use of bad rubbish' (the Womble family motto). Beresford linked up with the film company FilmFair, who commis-sioned Ivor Wood to animate and direct the series. The BBC Children's Department then bought in *The Wombles*, appointing Gra-hame Clutterbuck as producer. So this was not strictly a homegrown BBC product, but the Corporation showed flair in buying the series none the less, idiosyncratic as it was.

The Wombles are a hierarchical family with eccentric Great Uncle Bulgaria as its head, benignly ruling over Tobermory, Orinoco, Bungo, Tomsk and the rest of the clan. They are happy living on Wimbledon Common, but their disgust at the pollution from passing container lorries on the nearby motorways drives them to relocate elsewhere (underneath Hyde Park – which they discover to be a cornucopia of sticky wrapping papers and crisp packets). Children responded to these plump, hairy puppets with their 'cleaning-up' fervour, weird tartan shawls and peculiar headgear. By the mid-seventies schoolchildren themselves were picking up litter, following the family's lead, and the Wombles became the symbol for the 'Keep Britain Tidy' campaign. Rousing songs, composed by Mike Batt (such as 'Remember You're a Womble!') ensured that the creatures did not become too solemn.

The Wombles had a stirring comeback, organized by Mike Batt, at the Queen Mother's Birthday Parade on 18 July 2000, when a pop group dressed in Wombles 'Guardsmen' suits marched by the Royal Enclosure, provoking rare and unrestrained laughter in Prince Charles and others. I asked Mike Batt, who played Orinoco in the series, why he thought *The Wombles* struck such a chord with both adult and child viewers in 1973 and again in 1986. 'The British perceive themselves as being eccentric, so when they see a pop group composed of rodents dressed in Guardsmen's suits, their wildest hopes are confirmed,' he told me.

He was still busy with his Wombles compositions, writing new songs for the serial reissues. He recalls that when he first entered Wombledom, playing Orinoco, the one with the 'weight problem', he got a fan letter from an officer at an RAF station in South-East England telling him that all the officers had adopted Wombles names. 'I suppose becoming juvenile is one way to make a rough life more palatable,' Batt reflects. 'This Warrant Officer had taken the name of Orinoco. I think this is part of the everlasting appeal of some children's television series for grown-ups. It makes them feel young again – and also revives a time in their memories when they were small and carefree. It's a little like the bank manager who gets into jeans and does some rock 'n' roll at the disco.'

However, he expected the reissue of *The Wombles* to have a different effect on today's children watching it. 'When kids watched *The Wombles* in the seventies they certainly were inspired to keep their parks tidy, and they picked up litter in a cheerful way. But today, spoiling the environment has such serious overtones that it probably won't be viewed as light-heartedly, even by young children.'

The point Batt makes here, that children bring their own perceptions to television, is significant because it contradicts the common idea that children's minds have the consistency of litmus paper, passively absorbing whatever the tube projects. Research into their viewing habits and reactions provides strong evidence that the young do interact with television plots and characters. Telly-viewing, many child experts maintain, is a two-way process.

Whether this interaction is always healthy is another matter, especially when it comes to violence. Does the sight of brutality on the set inspire a child to commit imitative violence in real life? This conundrum has perplexed child experts since the dawn of children's television.[12] The debate was revived in the seventies by a rather eccentric science-fiction serial *The Incredible Hulk*, a US import originally based on a comic book character and first shown on CBS in 1978, purchased shortly afterwards by an independent company in the UK and very popular with both American and British children from eight to sixteen, especially boys.

The original story, which tells of a scientist who makes a horrible mistake in his laboratory while in search of the origins of human physical strength, was created by Stan Lee and adapted for television by Kenneth Johnson, who was also its executive producer. The plot centres on Dr David Banner, the story's enquiring scientist, played by actor Bill Bixby, who accidentally doses himself with gamma radiation. As a consequence, whenever placid Dr Banner becomes outraged, he metamorphoses into a large green creature with massive pectorals and a head of bushy hair like a miniature thatched cottage. The wrath of the creature (played by Lou Ferrigno) is eye-boggling: the swelling of the muscles, the apparent engorgement of the mouth and chin . . . These rages, lasting two minutes, were allowed to occur only twice in each sixty-minute episode. This was a marvellous device for creating suspense: the monster's rage was enormously satisfying as his body became swollen and his eyes went opaque (contact lenses helped actor Ferrigno with this particular transformation).

The excitement diminished when the creature's bland, do-gooding alter ego, David Banner, reappeared, busy with his benevolence: helping runaways from cruel institutions, alcoholics struggling to escape their habit and disabled stepchildren who were being slowly poisoned by their wicked step-parents, among others. His altruism was oceanic. Watching the programme with my son, then aged sixteen, I used to long for the moment when his attempts were thwarted so that he would have what came to be known by the production team as a 'Hulk-out'.

The effects on their children of watching the Hulk exploding into rage troubled some American parents, who wrote in to the producers saying that their children were imitating him when they became frustrated – 'blowing-out, growling, grunting and expanding their chests', wrote one. This worried the writer-producer, Jeff Freilich (there were eight producers in all over the three-year television stint, Freilich being one of the last). He expressed both his concerns and his authorial satisfaction in an interview:

What I found fascinating about the Hulk . . . and made me feel valuable as a writer, was that I got involved with a large number of child psychiatrists who thought that *The Hulk* was an outstanding children's program. The reason why was that it demonstrated to children, when Bill Bixby turned into Lou Ferrigno . . . that David Banner was acting out his anger, and that it was OK to become angry. Many children have a tremendous difficulty . . . expressing anger appropriately. I was told by a therapist that a lot of children, in a very healthy way, would become the Hulk when they became angry. Parents were complaining . . . not that they broke walls or stuff like that, but they'd growl . . . and throw pillows around. They would act out as if they were the Hulk. So I got concerned about that . . . At the time, I was particularly sensitive because I didn't want to be creating stories that would have really serious negative repercussions, particularly among children . . . [Therapists] at the Children's Hospital in Los Angeles . . . all said, 'When children act out anger, it's because they can't express it otherwise, and if they can't find a way to act it out it will become repressed, and if it does become repressed, they will grow into violent adults.'[13]

Freilich's comments were those of a lay thinker, not an expert, on the subject of child psychiatry and its relationship to television, but they are nevertheless fascinating because they reveal how television writers-cum-producers for children were becoming more sensitive to their young audiences' reactions.

The new seventies' attitude – that children should be considered seriously and given more thoughtful and weighty material – seemed to emerge simultaneously on both sides of the Atlantic without any apparent official coordination. *Sesame Street* had become the most popular children's show in the world, showing how it was possible to make a study of grammar, among other subjects, as much fun as a merry-go-round ride. Other US companies pitched their hats into the same ring and tried airing children's current affairs programmes, blending amusement and education. For example, CBS had its serious magazine show for children fashioned on *60 Minutes* (an in-depth documentary-cum-interview programme along the lines of the BBC's *Panorama*), called *30 Minutes*, and ABC created a programme called *After School Specials*, focusing on children's problems. It also broadcast another children's magazine show called *Kids Are People, Too*. The growth of serious afternoon and Saturday morning shows emerged from what had been a grab-bag of inexpensive cartoon shows and old Hollywood reruns such as *The Three Stooges*, *Laurel and Hardy* and *Lassie*.

Other countries that had hitherto ignored the serious side of children's television began to wake up. Australia, for instance, which had relied on 'bought in' children's programmes from the USA, Britain and France since 1952, created the Australian Children's Television Foundation in the seventies, a non-profit organization that produced programmes using the proceeds from the secondary sale of its original adult shows.[14]

One Australian serial that eclipsed all others in global popularity was *Skippy*, the story of a bush kangaroo, which aired in Britain in 1970 though it had been filmed originally in Australian from 1966 to 1968. Four years after it was made it was being screened in eighty countries worldwide. It was set in Waratah National Park outside Sydney and had Skippy helping out three young adolescent boys by warning them of potential danger with a 'tch tch tch tch' noise that enraptured young viewers (rather as Lassie's whines had done twenty years earlier). The idea that pets care passionately for their young masters and mistresses is an everlastingly popular theme and was enhanced in this case by the charms of an actual kangaroo.

The same formula propelled an American serial into international prominence in the sixties and early seventies. This was *Flipper*, the story of a female dolphin, called Mitzi in real life, who resided at the Dolphin Research Center in Grassy Key, Florida. Flipper, or Mitzi, while doing some spectacular leaps, also spent her time guarding her human masters, nudging their wayward boats to safety and making watery bellows to warn them of the approach of dangerous poachers. Of course the idea of a wild creature intent on protecting humans is pure romantic fantasy, but children did learn something about dolphins' habitats and the need to protect *them*. *Flipper*'s producer, Perry Katz, maintains that the series helped gain international recognition for the species. 'Flipper has come to symbolize ocean ecology,' he told one reporter.

The international popularity of *Skippy* and *Flipper* suggested that children were deeply appreciative of real animals as well as liking the stuffed variety. They were showing a taste for realism, even if the dolphin and kangaroo in the shows had been heavily anthropomorphized. This quest for realism was widely acknowledged and was discussed and hotly debated by creative people in the West, especially in the field of entertainment. In a *Time Out* interview in 1975 Malcolm McLaren, manager of the Sex Pistols,[15] trenchantly expounded his theory of the New Realism:

> The Sex Pistols are not a new 'fashion craze'; they're reality. Life is about concrete, the sinking pound, apathetic people and the highest unemployment figures ever. The Pistols are helping kids to think; that's why everybody's scared. They reflect life as it is in the council estates, not in the fantasy world that most rock artists create.[16]

His reference to council estates is an echo of a national obsession at the time. The sixties' dream that families would live blissfully in a Le Corbusier heaven, finding communal harmony in the tower blocks that were being built in city centres and suburbs alike, had become a nightmare. Parents felt alienated living in these honeycombed skyscrapers, and mothers trapped in their flats most of the day tended to spend more time worrying that their children might fall from a great height or be sexually molested in the playground than they did enjoying watching cloud formations from their windows. Millions of young mothers were becoming addicted to the tranquillizer Valium ('Mellow Yellow' in the rock jargon of the day).

Indeed, the seventies was the decade of disillusion in the West: Vietnam, Watergate, Nixon's impeachment, labour unrest in Britain (the 'Winter of Discontent'). It is not surprising, then, that the BBC, more sensitive to the beating of the national pulse than it was either previously or later on, decided to shake a little grit into its dramatic

95

mixing bowl. The result was *Grange Hill,* a dramatic serial depicting school life somewhere in the eastern suburbs of London, introduced in 1978. It was produced by the BBC's Drama Department under the auspices of Anna Home and aimed to show school life as it was experienced by working-class pre-teens and teenagers from the council estates. It dealt with contemporary issues in a fictional context: teenage pregnancy, drugs, bullying, violence, dyslexia, drinking. Anna Home wrote that the BBC 'wanted to get away from the world of Billy Bunter', by which she presumably meant fee-paying boarding-schools, merry jackanapes on the cricket ground and greedy raids on the tuck box.

The show was originally produced by Colin Cant, who established its abiding ethos of 'entertainment with a hard core'. To placate watchdog bodies such as the Broadcasting Standards Council, the characters were always to be shown suffering the proper consequences of their immoral actions; for instance, in one episode a bout of heavy drinking was followed by an a violently sick stomach, and the young imbiber was shown vomiting his heart out. At the same time the show aimed to be 'child-friendly'. Camera shots were taken at a deliberately low angle to give the drama a feel of 'audience ownership', to see, as one producer put it, 'school from a child's eyes'.

The serial was shot continuously at one studio, Elstree in outer London, and a group of young actors were kept on for lengthy periods to give the drama a feeling of solidity and continuity (much as in the long-running adult soaps today). The cast came from London stage schools such as the Italia Conti, the Corona and Anna Scher. It was a costly show for the BBC to make, as its producers had to abide by Home Office restrictions over hours so that the young actors could continue their real school studies. The show's first star was Todd Carty, who played the part of Tucker Jenkins in early *Grange Hill* episodes. Grown up now, he has been one of the star actors in *EastEnders*, playing the sympathetic character Mark Fowler. However, he was cruelly dropped from the soap in the summer of 2002 after a twelve-year stint.

In spite of the principle that wrong-doers should be shown suffering the consequences of their actions, children themselves sometimes expressed disapproval of behaviour depicted in *Grange Hill*.[17] One episode showed a fifteen-year-old taking drugs and regretting it finally because of the poor health it induced. Despite this, many thirteen- to fifteen-year-olds said they thought the episode *encouraged* drug-taking. Television producers were discovering that their young viewers' minds were not just blank screens, ready for the imprinting of insidious – or indeed benign – influences: children hold strong views of their own. This was a happy discovery in a an otherwise fairly unremittingly dour decade.

4

The Eighties

The Best and Worst of Children's Television

In May 1979 Britain welcomed to power its first woman Prime Minister, Margaret Thatcher, a leader who would shape and mould the ensuing decade. It is now almost impossible to think of the eighties without reflecting on this potent and voluble woman who made a 'market-led' economy based on monetarist policies sound like the only sort of government worth having.

The state of television in the eighties was healthy – 74 per cent of all UK households possessed a colour television set by this time – and the media entered into the spirit of the jockeying and jousting for commercial supremacy which characterized the decade. Channel 4 began broadcasting in 1982 with a heavy emphasis on advertising, and radio stations sprouted up like the heads of Hydra, all eagerly airing commercials.

The eighties also saw the rise of serious merchandising for children on both television and radio. It was suddenly discovered that an eye-catching, tuneful children's programme on film or television helped to market toys, that a 'My Little Pony' feature sold hundreds of thousands of little pink ponies with blond manes, complete with their own crenellated plastic stables (largely to girls: this is when manufacturers seemed first to wake up to the fact that toys could be gender-oriented;

boys, it appeared, preferred the weaponry of, say, the *Teenage Mutant Ninja Turtles*).

The realization by television film moguls and programme heads that children's media generated healthy revenue via toy merchandise might have heralded the end of quality programming for the under-twelves. Fortunately, this was not the case overall, though some abysmal animation serials spawning shoals of toys did come across the water from the US (the aggressive gear of the *Turtles* and the *Mighty Morphin Power Rangers* comes to mind).

Like Charles Dickens's 'best of times and worst of times', the eighties suffered some dreadful entertainment for children but also welcomed in a number of charming, witty animation series and thoughtful schools programmes, largely originating in Britain, as a product of the proliferation of commercial stations. For instance, Thames and Central Television commissioned a number of animated series and cartoons from Cosgrove Hall, the quality Disney-like cartoon studio at Chorlton-cum-Hardy, outside Manchester, such as the *Dangermouse* cartoons and animation series *The Wind in the Willows*.

The majority of parents were well enough able to handle the onslaught of advertising directed at their children. Except in the North and West of England, where the two largest heavy industries were in terminal decline, the eighties was a prosperous decade. Videos, cable television, CD players and home computers made their way into a large proportion of British homes. Between 1980 and 1989 the number of directors driving company cars rose by 20 per cent, and managers' pay more than doubled from £9,000 to £25,700 by mid-decade. Sixty per cent of households ran a car (the Ford Fiesta at £5,600 was the most popular) and each year nearly 2 million families holidayed in Spain, then the favourite holiday destination.[1] Not that the prosperity was evenly spread, but millions of citizens believed that some of it might rub off on them. Thousands of council-flat dwellers decided to buy their own flats, a Thatcherite dream that ended in heartache with the 1987 Stock Market crash and a sharp hike in interest rates to 14 per cent. However, until the late eighties there seemed to be plenty of money around. It is small wonder, then, that Harry Enfield's comic character, the working-class yuppie Loadsamoney, later became a cult figure (first appearing on BBC 1's *Saturday Night Live* in 1990).

Granada Television was the favourite commercial company in those days. Its *Coronation Street* was the clear victor in the soap-viewing wars – even against strong competition from imported soaps, notably *Dallas* and *Dynasty* from the USA and *Neighbours* from Australia. Granada also managed to give the BBC a cultural black eye with two dramatic serials, *Brideshead Revisited*, based on the Evelyn Waugh novel, and *The Jewel in the Crown*, the elegiac saga tracing the end of the British Raj in India. The partnership of Sir Denis Forman, Granada's managing director, and Sidney Bernstein (Lord Bernstein), its chairman, appeared unbeatable.

The BBC fought a holding action in the eighties, neither failing nor particularly excelling (as it had in the sixties and seventies with serials such as *The Forsyte Saga* and *The Onedin Line*). Its two star children's shows, *Blue Peter* and *Grange Hill*, continued to please young audiences but tended to cling unadventurously to their original formats. The Corporation was in a rather difficult position *vis-à-vis* Prime Minister Thatcher. She was no great admirer of public service broadcasting and subscribed to the prevailing Conservative view that the BBC was riddled with Lefties inimical to her rule. As Hugo Young writes in his biography of the Iron Lady: 'Mrs Thatcher's direct criticisms [of the BBC] may have been relatively infrequent, but there was an undertow of impatience when television failed to see its role as being precisely concordant with government policy . . . What this amounted to was a form of intimidation of a kind.' Young goes on to say that the Tories, guided by Norman Tebbit, subtly forced a reorganization upon the BBC. 'The net effect', he writes, 'was to erode the confidence of the broadcasters.'[2] The commercial channels were not susceptible to this kind of pressure, though they did face plenty of criticism: Margaret Thatcher pronounced the new Channel 4's news coverage 'unsound', for instance.

One other new station, TV-am, got off to a creaking, juddering start on 17 January 1983. TV-am was Britain's first breakfast show, and its struggle for survival until it met an ignominious end in the late eighties afforded Britain much entertainment. The company, based at Camden Lock in north-west London, opened in a blaze of glory and brandishing a group of star presenters known as the 'Famous Five' (*pace* Enid Blyton): Michael Parkinson, Robert Kee, Anna Ford, Angela Rippon and Esther Rantzen. In spite of their celebrity and personal expertise, the breakfast show did not really take off. Experts blame the poor integration between script and line editors and the presenters themselves. Union regulations meant that line-cutters were highly paid for overtime work, so management allowed feature items to go sloppily unedited, tending to run too long, rather than pay the overtime rates. This was an especially bad idea for breakfast television, which needed to move crisply between time slots because viewers like to time their morning routines with items they know will be screened at regular points.

Anna Ford and Angela Rippon were fired during the first year – spicy news for the tabloids, reaching a satisfying climax when Anna Ford threw a glass of white wine over Jonathan Aitken, the company's major shareholder, at a chic London cocktail party given shortly after her dismissal. The late Auberon Waugh celebrated the event in the *Daily Mail* with a column on the 'Best Throwing Wines'.

The chronicler of this saga, journalist Michael Leapman, suggests that the Independent Broadcasting Authority (IBA) was blinded by the glitter of the 'Famous Five' when it took the decision to award the breakfast television franchise to TV-am. If so, this is an object lesson in 'how not to run a television station'. Successful television has as much to do with the technicians as it does with the stars – technology *is* the message, to paraphrase Marshall McLuhan. But whatever the truth of TV-am's demise, its immediate relevance to the history of children's television lies in the peculiar fact that the station was briefly saved, in the summer of 1983, by the appearance of a puppet handled by David Claridge. This was Roland Rat.[3]

When Greg Dyke, an Australian, took over the sinking company in early July 1983, six months after its launch, he knew he had to take drastic action if he was to reverse the company's flagging fortunes. Fresh from his native land where breakfast television flourished, he knew that viewing figures rose in the summer when children were home for the holidays and tuning in at breakfasttime. Accordingly, he extended *Good Morning, Britain* to three hours' duration, lengthened the commercials so they tended to break into the feature items less frequently, ran competitions, had presenters read out winning Bingo numbers, featured bosomy blonde actress Diana Dors talking about diets, and introduced two puppets, Roland Rat and Kevin the Gerbil. This was 'dumbing down' with a vengeance (long before the term was coined), and it worked. TV-am's viewing figures nearly doubled from 1 million in late July to 1.75 million in mid-August 1983, half a million more viewers than the BBC attracted at breakfast time in the same week.

The press loved the turn-around in TV-am's fortunes: it was a headline writer's dream, generating predictable jokes about rats 'saving' rather than 'abandoning' sinking ships. Even *The Times* pitched in with a solemn editorial headed 'A Rat to the Rescue': the IBA had 'failed in its statutory duty as the public's guardian of quality', it intoned.[4]

But what exactly *had* happened? Had summer madness so gripped adult viewers at breakfast time that they were mesmerized by a sardonic, leather-capped rat in dark glasses prone to drawling 'Yeahhhhhh'? In retrospect, this seems to have been another case of 'kidult' viewing – the shared pleasure by parents and children of an entertainment feature, puppet or animated cartoon. Roland Rat, like some knowing street gang leader, delighted fathers and sons, mothers and daughters alike. His irreverent, cheeky know-it-all attitude was irresistible, especially in the morning when the family throat was still furred and impulses were slow.

Besides, cheekiness was a prized commodity in the eighties, especially when it was directed by a puppet at a distinguished member of the arts or society. *The Muppets* was Number One in the cheekiness stakes. This thirty-minute show first aired on ATV in 1976, but by 1981 it had acquired one of the highest ratings for any programme, children's or adult's. The stars were Jim Henson's brilliant soft puppets: Kermit the Frog, Fozzie Bear, The Great Gonzo, Wayne and Wanda and of course the seductive Miss Piggy. The scripts were written by Jack Burns, Marc London, Jerry Juhl and Henson himself. Each programme featured a well-known human who was ensnared in the Muppets' zany antics. One of these famous 'victims' was Peter Ustinov. Talking about his appearance with them, he says: 'People warn actors not to go on screen or stage with children or pets. To that I would add puppets. Audiences only have eyes for them.'

One of the most famous *Muppets* scenes starred Miss Piggy interrupting the great Russian ballet dancer, Rudolph Nureyev, taking a shower. With her porcine features, flapping eyelashes, Brigitte Bardot hairdo and all-round explosive sex appeal, she makes a concerted effort to seduce him in his half-clad state. What was wonderful about Miss Piggy was that she was such a throwback, ignoring the bra-burning feminism of the previous decades in favour of eye-batting, man-eating outrageousness. That she should be exercising her farmyard charms on a 'glad-to-be-gay' world-famous dancer only made the scene more memorable. (Several minutes of this episode were repeated in Channel 4's *The 100 Best Kids' TV Shows* in August 2001; *The Muppets* came second in the popularity poll, after *The Simpsons*.) Four Muppets movies were made in 1979, 1981, 1984 and 1992, and while they were quietly enjoyable they lacked the knock-about charms of the sassy Henson creations shown on the small screen.

Other beguiling puppets appeared on Thames Television's *Rainbow*, a half-hour children's programme that vied with the BBC's *Play School* in its attempts to combine education with entertainment for the under-tens. *Rainbow*'s most original puppets were an orange metal round-head with a huge zippered mouth called Zippy, a pink hippo called George and a big bear named Bungle. The threesome were mischievous and irreverent, especially to their 'parent', the presenter Geoffrey Hayes. Hayes had his work cut out trying to moderate the threesome's saucy behaviour – telling them how to treat their peers, when to go to bed, why they should share and so on. *Rainbow* was the first British programme to show puppets and humans interacting in a significant way, though the formula was familiar from America's *Sesame Street*, where Oscar the Grouch and Big Bird were frequently given gentle lectures on behaviour by humans on the show.

Although British parents in the eighties were tolerant of low-brow rodents and pink hippos making wisecracks over breakfast and afternoon tea, and they were quite willing to buy replicas of them to put in their children's Christmas stockings, many were increasingly unhappy about two nakedly toy-based programmes purchased from the USA, the *Mighty Morphin Power Rangers* and *Teenage Mutant Ninja Turtles*. In both serials, which featured humans (often teenagers) and robots, there was a crude sales pitch hidden not too far below the surface.

In the latter, bought by the BBC and thus shown without direct television advertising, the salesmanship was done through advertisements in other media. There was an emphasis on weaponry and aggressive fighting – karate chops and vicious kicks – that appealed to young boys. There was a pretence that good triumphed over bad (both Turtles and Power Rangers fought sinister alien invaders), but wary parents and suspicious child psychiatrists were sure that these shows had been made with sales in mind rather than the promotion of altruism.

Child studies in North America, Britain and Europe were beginning to alarm teachers and parents about the effect that television's glorification of violence might have on the behaviour of the young. Today we are used to reading about imitative violence,[5] but in the eighties this was a new and shocking idea. One report in a US broadcasting journal in 1979 of studies of the behaviour of young adolescents had a particular impact. Surveys of youngsters' viewing habits suggested that an already aggressive young person would prefer programmes that contained violence:

> Evidence supporting the thesis that aggressive predispositions may underlie the enjoyment of violent television content has emerged from several studies. In one of these, a panel of young people was surveyed twice across a period of one year. Measures of their attitudes toward the use of aggression and their television viewing habits over time were taken . . . evidence did emerge that individuals who exhibited aggressive attitudes at the beginning of the study expressed particularly strong preferences for violent programming after one year.[6]

So parents had two reasons to dislike the *Ninja Turtles* and the *Power Rangers* – they disliked being strong-armed into buying repulsive replicative toys from the series, and now there was growing concern that the karate chops being noisily mimicked by their ten-year-olds in the living-room might result in future acts of violent crime.

Ninja Turtles was first broadcast in 1984. Whether their creators had in the forefront of their minds the goal of producing cult figures that would sell merchandise, we do not know. The series was based on stories by Kevin Eastman, featuring four turtles with the names of Renaissance artists who love pizza, live in New York sewers, are time travellers and like the martial arts as well as flying kites with children – it sounds like good fun, doesn't it? *Power Rangers* was in some ways similar, except that the main characters were five fairly normal teenagers dressed in bright, satiny football garb with matching metallic helmets. They were also time travellers (*Dr Who* started something), had magical powers, liked the martial arts and defeated evil aliens (metal robots usually, with scary headgear and pop eyes on skewers). The merchandise spawned by these series consisted largely of copies of the menacing artefacts the characters carried and wore – helmets, swords, masks, spears, rifles, daggers, machetes. The stuff was sold via multiple franchisees throughout the world. (I watched a home video of *Teenage Mutant Ninja Turtles III*, a late nineties' film made by Twentieth Century Fox about the Turtles fighting samurai warriors in feudal Japan – PG rated – and I noticed that the name of the outlet selling the swords in Japan is listed in the final credits.)

The explosion of such merchandising was a direct result of the substantial deregulation of US children's television by the Federal Communications Commission (FCC) in 1984. The leading characters in such programmes could now be advertised directly after the show with a lengthy commercial. In 1991 the FCC reversed this general edict, restricting advertisements to ten and a half minutes an hour at weekends and twelve minutes an hour on weekdays, but by then the damage had been done.

Voicing his concern over these two programmes, Iowa State University marketing study expert Dr Russ Laczniak told a conference in 1995:

> Young children have had little time to build a sufficient defense against advertising. They can't distinguish the selling intent of the commercial. Therefore, they have the potential to be exploited as consumers. Children are even more defenseless against toy-based programs.
>
> Even if children are able to detect that the purpose of a thirty-second commercial is to sell something, they don't recognize the same intentions in a half-hour program.[7]

The fact that the BBC bought and screened the *Ninja Turtles*, changing its title to *Teenage Mutant Hero Turtles* to play down the martial-arts aspect, tarnished the halo it was occasionally guilty of boasting about in the past (though Anna Home insists that there was no selling of *Turtles'* spin-off toys by the Corporation during her time as head of Children's Programmes). The show was slotted into the Saturday morning children's hour, *Going Live*. By the end of the eighties the child audience for the *Ninja Turtles* reached 5 million in Britain, though by that time the BBC had toned down some of its more violent content. They also made sure that presenters cautioned young viewers not to try to descend into sewers as their Turtle heroes did. None the less, quite a few under-tens *were* discovered stuck in drains and sewers around the country: in September 1990, for instance, police reported children being trapped underground from Leeds to London and Hertfordshire. Happily, there were no fatalities.

American imports did not have a monopoly on bad taste in this era. One year into its existence in 1983, Channel 4 produced a grotesque show called *Mini-Pops* in which under-tens were invited to sing numbers and pose as their favourite pop idols. The sight of one curly-headed little girl gyrating slinkily around the stage as Diana Ross has found a niche in television history, since it was included by Channel 4 itself in September 2000 in *100 Worst TV Moments*. Well, they said it.

The BBC was still providing a prestigious service for children, despite putting on the nasty *Turtles* – and then, even more embarrassingly, acquiring such huge ratings for them. *Blue Peter*, under the guidance of Biddy Baxter, flourished as ever. The young woman presenter, Janet Ellis, captivated audiences, especially when she achieved a record for the longest civilian free-fall parachute jump from a plane in 1987, an event thrillingly filmed at close quarters.

Thames Television maintained strong competition to *Blue Peter* with *Magpie,* a live magazine programme for eight- to fourteen-year-olds. Marilyn Gaunt, now a distinguished freelance documentary-maker, was a trainee director for *Magpie* at Teddington, outside London, and remembers the excitement of working on a live show as something of a novice. 'We had the feeling that *Blue Peter* was stuck in the fifties,' she told me. 'We didn't make ships out of shoe boxes and glue toilet rolls together with sticky plaster, and our presenters didn't portray themselves as friendly brothers and sisters. Presenter Mark Robertson was handsome – someone the young teenage girls had crushes on – he looked like Marc Bolan. We aimed to educate, all right, but it was education with a bounce. If we wanted to show kids how plumbing worked, for instance, we'd throw some bubble bath into the bath we were filming.' Marilyn worked non-stop, shooting features in the mornings with a crew of eight and then filming the live show in the studio in the afternoons. For their feature items they liked 'OBs', she says – outside broadcasts – and the further outside the studio the better. On one occasion, in order to show children the inside workings of a hotel, she penetrated the bowels of London's Hilton Hotel on Park Lane, showing presenter Jenny Hanley prowling through the kitchens and laundry rooms.

'Fifty per cent of our show consisted of feature items that had either been filmed on location on previous days or were recorded on the morning or afternoon of the show during rehearsal time. The rest was live. Our presenters wanted to give a strong impression of sharing things, of being enthusiastic – the dearest wish was that the enthusiasm would transmit itself.'

Magpie was extremely successful, but at the end of 1980 Thames Television cancelled it because of union troubles. Marilyn saw both good and bad in unions. 'There *were* restrictive practices,' she explains. 'We had to work within certain hours. If you extended over the lunch-hour, you'd be in trouble. It was pretty much *verboten*. On the other hand, the union rules meant young people were trained as part of the job both in the studio and on the outside broadcasts because a regulation number of people were required for a crew. I used to have eight people helping out then – now I'm lucky if I have two. If a young person wants to learn to be a film-maker now, he or she won't get the training free on the job as they did then. Today a trainee has to become a runner or go to a film school to gain any experience.'

Marilyn believes children are quite capable of differentiating between reality and fantasy on television. 'I think we underestimate children's ability to distinguish between the two,' she says. 'If they could-n't identify what is real, I suppose they would be steam-rollering over their cats after watching *Tom and Jerry*, and we know that they don't.'[8]

The conviction that one should not patronize children was taking a firm grip on programme-makers by the mid-eighties, and some pro-grammes were becoming positively sophisticated.

The BBC's story-reading series, *Jackanory*, a fifteen-minute fixture in the afternoon schedule that had been running since the mid-sixties and continued until 1992, selected tales by well-loved authors. Two such works were by Ted Hughes and Roald Dahl, read by Rik Mayall and Tom Baker (the former Dr Who). Rik Mayall's reading of Dahl's story about a little boy who attempts to kill his granny, *George's Marvellous Medicine*, reverberated around Britain to the horror of parents, while Baker's recounting of Hughes's *The Iron Man*, with its metal giant who eats wire fences like spaghetti and pops a 'greasy black stove into his mouth like a toffee' received mixed reviews, too.[9, 10]

Jackanory was a brilliant idea, with its star performers reading the classics and thus whetting children's appetites for books. Over the years its readers included Joyce Grenfell, Judi Dench, Alan Bennett, Geraldine McEwan and James Robertson Justice. The two actors who performed the most often over the twenty-five years were Bernard Cribbins (111 programmes) and Kenneth Williams (69 programmes).

Jackanory was not the only children's television series based on good books for the under-twelves. Willis Hall and Keith Waterhouse adapted Barbara Euphan Todd's *Worzel Gummidge* for Southern Television in the late seventies. By 1981 it had become a roaring hit. The stars of the series, Jon Pertwee (of *Dr Who* fame) and Una Stubbs (who had starred in *Till Death Us Do Part* as Alf Garnett's beleaguered daughter Rita), enhanced an already intriguing storyline about scarecrows at Scatterbrook Farm in Yorkshire. The series went out in the traditional Sunday afternoon children's drama slot.

Hall and Waterhouse took some liberties with the original Todd characters, making Worzel into an aggressive scarecrow with pointy nose and mean lips instead of the benign country bumpkin of the book. They also converted his Aunt Sally (his actual aunt in the story) into his sweetheart. Una Stubbs was magical in the role, making the jerky scarecrow movements and head-bobbing lectures to both children and lover seem very robotic indeed. A straw cloche hat set off her painted features, and she somehow managed to seem more wood and straw than human flesh.

In the bewildering way of television, this highly popular series was axed at the height of its success in 1981 when Southern Television lost its franchise. Subsequent attempts to revive the series both in Ireland and in New Zealand were unsuccessful.

Another unpatronizing series for children aged eight to ten was Granada Television's programme for schools, *Picture Box*, which had begun in 1966 and lasted through the eighties. It offered particularly good viewing in its later stages when the attractive, soft-voiced presenter, Alan Rothwell, a former *Coronation Street* actor, performed. The camera work was top rate and production values high. John Coop, the producer, was determined to give young minds and primary school teachers the best teaching tips throughout the ITV network – which comprised thirteen companies in Ulster, Scotland, Wales and East Anglia. The tools of learning were often original feature films combined with book lists and topics presented in the form of eclectic questions on aesthetic themes: 'What is rhythm?', 'How does lighting affect art?', 'What is a scrap yard?', 'What is often unique about every-

day objects?' *Picture Box* was the forerunner of present-day art appreciation and instruction shows such as *Art Attack*.

Sybil Marshall, the programme's educational adviser for twenty-
three years, said to me recently: 'Do look at one of our videos – the one
point a video would make better is our absolute refusal, on principle,
to "talk down" to the children.' I took her advice, and concede her
point! One of their feature films in particular took my eye – a fifteen-
minute photographic essay on a scrap yard. The camera played on
rusty fenders and crumpled car bonnets, revealing berry-covered
brambles and creamy cowslips snaking through broken windscreens. It
could have been put on at the National Film Theatre on the South
Bank as a choice example of cinematography.

Animated puppet series in the tradition of the sixties' *Trumptonshire* flourished in the eighties as well. Three fine series were made:
Thomas the Tank Engine (Thames Television), *Postman Pat* (BBC;
created by Ivor Wood) and *Fireman Sam* (Channel 4). All three series
are set in rural villages in England and Wales and have leading men
who revere their own mode of transport (Postman Pat's love affair with
his van is shared by a useless cat who sits by his side). Fireman Sam, a
dedicated fighter of fires, adores his fireman's helmet and fire engine
but has one serious problem – there aren't many fires around to put out
in the pastoral heaven he inhabits. Repetitive jingles are used, funny
hats and wigs reappear along with snout noses (Postman Pat has quite
a hooter), and there is the dedication to the job which gripped the
Trumptonshire mob as well. We are back to the stop-frame animation
technique and the ensuing jerky walks which also thrived in *Camberwick Green* and pleased the under-fives.

Pre-schoolers seem to delight in certain features: repetitive jingles,
familiar puppet routines (for example, Fireman Sam's fire helmet
drops on to his head via a pulley at his front door as he pushes a but-
ton; this act is performed at the beginning of each episode);
catchphrases; showy personal habits (Bella Lasagna, the Italian café

owner in *Fireman Sam*, loves making endless cappuccinos, for example).

Thomas the Tank Engine, based on the forties' stories of an Isle of Man vicar, the Reverend W. Awdry, which he wrote and recited to his bed-ridden son, was the greatest surprise. There were no sinister attempts to commercialize its simple and happy narrative of engines thundering around a seaside village, yet it became a tremendous marketing success, the progenitor of thousands of books and toy trains. Most astonishing of all, it was a huge success in the USA, starting a new reverse trend – that of American companies purchasing British children's television. Nickelodeon, the US-based cable channel owned by Music Television – MTV – purchased *Dangermouse* at the same time.

Dangermouse was the successful creation of Mark Hall and Brian Cosgrove, whose cartoon centre outside Manchester bears their names. Dangermouse was a cheeky chap who dressed all in white and swore his outfit was *not* thermal underwear but pure Savile Row (Cosgrove and Hall point out that a white suit was a much cheaper option for a cartoon character in any case, colour being expensive). *Dangermouse* was a spoof of the James Bond films; it was aired on Thames Television from 1981 to 1992 in 160 episodes. Dangermouse's sidekick, Penfold, a bespectacled mongrel, made a good foil and was given to proclaiming 'Oo-'eck!' in the unmistakable voice of actor Terry Scott. Dangermouse himself had the street-wise voice of David Jason ('Good grief!'). The inclusion of such famous television voices added enormously to the appeal of the series.

Since the days of Mickey, a smark-aleck mouse stands a good chance of success . . . but a train? The makers of *Thomas the Tank Engine* – Britt Allcroft had adapted the stories for television – seem to have inadvertently hit on something significant: children love the anthropomorphizing of stuffed animals, but they also delight in the humanizing of machines. The various trains, tanks and engines – Thomas the Tank, George the Steamroller, Caroline the Red Car,

Percy the Diesel and Toby the Small Engine – are all awash with emotion. Thomas himself is fearful (his rolling eyes denote his nervousness at being late); Ben's iron mouth droops when he's in pain; Bill, one half of a twin engine, looks cross when he quarrels with his twin. They are all terrified of the Fat Controller, a pompous Yorkshireman who fusses about winning the 'Best-Dressed Station' award.

Another puppet animation series which Thames Television broadcast in 1987 also came from Cosgrove Hall. This was Kenneth Grahame's *The Wind in the Willows*. I watched the production team making the 'Toad of Toad Hall' sequence in 1987 at Cosgrove Hall and was astounded by the meticulous care the team took with the puppets' clothes and possessions. One art graduate working on the team had taken two months to find and make the right motor cycle for Toad. She wanted it to be 'flashy', she said, to suit Toad's exhibitionistic character, but it also had to look like a true 1907 model. This had sent her trawling through the exhibition halls of Manchester. She eventually settled on a period machine which 'suited Toad's inflated ego', she said.

This version of *The Wind in the Willows* was a ground-breaking show in many ways. The puppets 'spoke' their lines – a complicated procedure as their wooden mouths had to synchronize with their words. This was done by fitting joints in the puppets' mouths which caused them to open and shut. They had Ratty speak, for instance, by putting a screwdriver in his ear to operate the joints – an undignified but effective measure.

By the end of the eighties children's television had evolved into a global business, and it had also become a minor art form. Who was going to triumph – the business moguls and international merchandisers, or the creative artists? It would be a close race. Sometimes – the launching of the BBC's *Teletubbies* is one such occasion – both sides won. In any case, children's television entertainment had moved light-years away from the humble wooden click-clacking of hooves on a piano top of *Muffin the Mule*.

5

The Nineties

Soul-Searching, Unexpected Successes and 'Kidult' Viewing

The early nineties found children's television programme-makers and those overseeing broadcasting standards for young viewers in a mood of near desperate soul-searching. Had they, in their excitement at producing neo-realism for schoolchildren, gone overboard and reached beyond reasonable standards of propriety? In USA, such questions were often raised by regulatory bodies such as the Federal Communications Commission. In UK it was the BBC that was examining its own conscience.

The deepest worry, as so often where children are concerned, was about the young viewers' exposure to adult sexuality. In the late eighties and early nineties a goodly number of explicitly sexual movies had been screened: oral sex had featured in early eighties' films as *The Postman Always Rings Twice* and *Dressed to Kill* (ones that moved Mary Whitehouse, the voice of the National Viewers' and Listeners' Association, to comment that 'if they didn't show it on the screen, most people wouldn't know about oral sex'),[1] and a brutal rape scene featured in Quentin Tarantino's *Reservoir Dogs*. These films were all X- or 18-rated, but they were widely discussed and featured in television clips, and information about them – however partially understood – would have trickled down to the young.

One programme-maker who was deeply disturbed by the climate of permissiveness was Edward Barnes, a BBC children's director who succeeded Monica Sims in the late seventies and who had initially brought Phil Redmond's *Grange Hill* to the screen in 1978 (it lasted until 1996 and was reintroduced in 2001 in its usual half-hourly format). In 1991 the programme tackled pupil pregnancy and abortion, arousing Mary Whitehouse's ire once again. But it also pricked Barnes's conscience. In 1997, looking back on his four-year reign as director of children's programmes, Barnes told one interviewer:

> I've often wondered if I wasn't in some way responsible for artificially bringing children into teenage, adult and sexual values before the time they were needed . . . I think that it is the effect of ramming sexual values and of some kinds of values that surround sexuality down people's throats before they've reached puberty. I think it is not a good idea really, because that is eroding childhood. And I sometimes wonder if I've been a party to that in some way.[2]

In the Victorian era few people worried much about how to treat children, emotionally or physically. In fact, children were cruelly exploited in the mines and factories of early nineteenth-century Britain and America, valued for their small size and manual dexterity. The children of the poor had to prove themselves 'useful'. They were sent up chimneys from the age of five, for example, suffering lung cancer and damaged eyesight. In the mills of 1840, children were highly valued for their ability to creep around the floors of cotton factories picking up cotton waste. In the factories and sweatshops of North America, from Maine to Manhattan, children of nursery school age were placed in women's accessory workshops to string beads on slippers, purses and fancy hats. In coastal US towns in New England children worked at canning herrings for eleven or twelve hours a day. Their little fingers were also used to wrap brown papers around 'stogies' in cigar factories.

Such cruelty and exploitation continued well into the twentieth century, until children's rights reformers and concerned citizens won the battle to introduce child labour laws and punishments for parents who treated children cruelly. In Britain it was not until 1933 that the Children and Young Persons Act made a child's 'unnecessary suffering' at the hands of a parent a misdemeanour.[3]

Thus the idea that childhood deserved special protection did not really take root until shortly before the Second World War; and the concept that they should have entertainment of their own was entirely new (good books for children had been written before this, but they normally only reached the middle classes). So BBC Radio's *Children's Hour*, introduced in the forties, and then television's *Watch With Mother* of the fifties were truly revolutionary. The BBC's golden rule in those times was to keep programmes 'safe and cheerful', a clear reaction against the depredations of the past.

So when the pendulum began to swing away from child protection towards ever more explicit realism, it is not surprising that sensitive broadcasters such as Edward Barnes should be disturbed. Were children not becoming overburdened with depictions of sex and violence that they could neither comprehend nor absorb? Adult sexuality, the simulated sex of situation comedies and crime dramas, was being watched by under-tens. How many parents, after all, were holding to the nine o'clock evening 'watershed'[4] and forbidding their children to view television after bedtime, especially at weekends? Was this not a new kind of abuse? In the early nineties regulatory bodies on both sides of the Atlantic began to wake from their torpor.

This global shudder of revulsion at the state of children's broadcasting grew with each year. Canada, a nation that had always been sensitive to the possibility that television might corrupt children, was perhaps the most vigilant. The Canadian Broadcasting Standards Council (CBSC) began gathering complaints from its members in 1991 and by the end of that year had collected 645 complaints on sex-role portrayal, discrimination and television violence. (Again the *Mighty Morphin Power Rangers* collected a sizeable raft of complaints.) The CBSC was an impressive organization, composed as it was of broadcasters themselves. It included 320 radio stations, sixty-one television stations and two French/English networks. It established three codes to be administered by its members – the Sex Portrayal Code, the Violence Code and the Code of Ethics.

New Zealand had always been a cautious purchaser of children's programmes, and was normally satisfied with its supply from the BBC, in particular, but it was having doubts about some US imports. In 1991 its self-regulatory body, the Broadcasting Standards Authority, published a paper entitled 'Television Violence: An Analysis of the Portrayal of Violent Acts on Three New Zealand Broadcasting Television Channels During the Week of 11th–17th February'.[5]

Disquiet in the USA was revealed at this time not so much through governmental action or parental regulation (this came later with the V-chip,[6] which would allow parents to block programmes electronically if they deemed them unsuitable for their offspring) but through the protests of individuals. A popular book of the time said it all in its title: this was Marie Winn's *The Plug-In Drug*.[7] Newton N. Minow, who had called television a 'vast wasteland' in a book in 1961, wrote another in 1995 saying it was still a wasteland, possibly more like Siberia than ever.[8] This was perhaps a poor time for the Republican majority in the US Senate, led by Robert Dole, to demand that the Public Broadcasting Service (PBS) stop relying on federal appropriations to fund its children's programming. 'It's nauseating', said Peggy Charren of the advocacy group Action for Children's Television (ACT), 'that the same guy [Dole] who is attacking what's terrible for children's television is working very hard to keep the alternatives from the screen.'

Keith Spicer, chairman of the Canadian Radiotelevision and Telecommunication Commission, added to the outcry by declaring television responsible for violence in society. As he put it: 'For the last twenty years, there has been one overriding finding . . . the mass media are significant contributors to the aggressive behaviour and aggression-related attitudes of many children, adolescents and adults.'[9]

Britain responded rather laconically to this upsurge of concern, but the government did wake up and create a polite watchdog body, the Broadcasting Standards Council (BSC), in 1989, with a committee chaired by the editor and journalist William Rees-Mogg. The BSC began by commissioning research papers on television's effects and organizing discussion groups at The Sanctuary near Parliament Square, Westminster. Its aims were to set standards and ensure fairness in broadcasting, radio and television, to produce codes of practice, consider and adjudicate on complaints and monitor standards. Its aims and codes were set out formally in 1996 when it became an official statutory body.

In the early nineties I regularly attended meetings of media journalists, usually convened by Rees-Mogg. The late Jim Bredin, head of Border Television in the eighties, was another frequent participant. 'These are the politest damned people I've ever met!' Jim protested amiably to me after one meeting. Perhaps this extreme courtesy and restraint sprang from a desire not to seem too rabid. These low-key discussions often focused on imitative violence, and whether it actually existed. Most of the group appeared to believe that it did not. (But this was before the April 1999 Columbine High School Massacre in Denver, Colorado, where the adolescent killers Eric Harris and Dylan Klebold were said to be followers of the morbid 'shock-rocker' Marilyn Manson, who allegedly glorified violent death in his songs.) The Council's main concern so far as children were concerned was that the nine o'clock watershed was being widely ignored. As one BSC paper on children's viewing habits reported, quoting an eleven-year-old girl who watched television as and when she liked: 'I use headphones on my own television. My parents don't know it takes headphones.'[10]

Watchdog bodies around the world were also troubled by the multiplicity of choice that burst upon the viewing public in the late eighties and early nineties. The newly arrived video cassette recorder allowed audiences to save their favourite programmes and watch them at any time; they could also rent a wide variety of video games; and they could subscribe to satellite and cable television channels. Reasonably affluent families who could afford satellite television now had access to Nickelodeon, which offered an all-day menu of some of the best of children's animation serials such as *The Rugrats*. 'This means,' commented the ACT's Peggy Charren, 'that poor kids – with the exception of their being able to receive *Sesame Street* – are getting the worst television, they who need good television the most.'[11]

The sheer quantity of programming now available provoked mockery as well as concern in some quarters. Adults caught up in the tentacles of television were dubbed 'tubeheads' by a Vancouver grass-roots organization called the Media Foundation. This group launched a vivid poster campaign showing 'tubeheads' wrestling to get television sets off their heads.[12] They and others believe that television addiction is a major health issue of our times.

Such concerns about the effects of over-exposure to television are reasonable, but it is doubtful that scaremongering will make the problems go away. There is also a danger of overlooking the positive benefits of television access. In the winter of 2000 *Newsweek* ran a picture and caption of a plump Russian grandmother in her small kitchen bemoaning the loss of television reception (following electrical supply failure in Moscow). She desperately missed the news at night, she said. television is one of the truly affordable windows on the world and one which few, particularly those of limited means, can afford to be without. The recent struggles between ITV and the BBC to dominate the ten o'clock news slot demonstrate how well they understand the importance of a feature that is both an entertainment attraction and a genuine educational tool.

Increasingly fierce competition between the television companies forced them to streamline their management structures, merge with other companies and seek international merchandising outlets. They also radically reduced the size of their core staffs in the late eighties and early nineties, switching to a system of mandatory outside commissioning. The BBC's seven-storey Leviathan covering three acres in White City, west London, and Granada's headquarters in central Manchester, in which huge studios churned out glitzy entertainment programmes, are both now pretty much ancient history. Executive offices still abound, of course, and conference rooms exude the aroma of coffee and the murmur of shareholders, accountants and directors, but the creative work of dreaming up new serials and sitcoms is now mostly 'outsourced'.

Many regret the change. Marjorie Giles, now retired, was a staff and freelance producer at Granada for over twenty years, producing the local morning programme for ethnic minorities, *This Is Your Right*; she told me: 'The feeling of a central nervous system, of a communal heartbeat, was one of the most exciting things about working at Granada in the sixties and seventies. I guess the canteen was the real centre. Along with the clattering of knives and forks went a lot of behind-your-cupped-hands conspiratorial discussion of your ideas for programmes. If you distrusted someone, you kept mum over your lunchtime platter, but if you didn't you would sit there and divulge all – sharing ideas, themes, feelings about colleagues and so on. I went back to Granada recently and I couldn't believe it! There were only a few "suits" around in the corridors and – most stunning of all – no canteen. Quite shocking.'

The creation in 1979 of BBC Enterprises Ltd, a subsidiary company wholly owned by the BBC, marked a giant step towards a market-led international strategy. Offices were set up in Australia and Canada, with distributors in the USA, Japan and South America. By 1982 turnover had increased from £234,000 in 1960 to £23 million.

Television sales accounted for 70 per cent of annual turnover. The money was all to be fed back into the coffers of the BBC itself.[13] But expansion internationally led to reductions at home. By 1990 four thousand Home Services staff had been made redundant. Three years later a far-reaching policy called 'Producer Choice' was introduced. BBC television programme-makers now had to commission a quarter of all their programmes from independent producers. Internal services, staff, film crews and facilities were all drastically cut as a result.

It is difficult not to feel sentimental about the passing of the old BBC, the nation's pride and as English as a Bath bun, summed up for me in the image of Dorothea Brooking creating stunning children's dramas in derelict courtyards in the suburbs of London. However, far from damaging the quality of children's programming, 'outsourcing' could offer exciting possibilities for those who knew where to look. In fact, BBC producers had been commissioning from outside in a small way since the golden age of *Bagpuss* and *The Clangers* in the early seventies. But now, for the BBC and commercial companies alike, producers were as good as their contact books.

One of the most rewarding addresses to have in your book belonged to a 63-year-old children's programme-maker living in Warwickshire named Anne Wood. Luckily for the BBC, someone in the children's department had remembered to jot it down, for she was the creator of *Teletubbies*.

The Teletubbies are four furry dolls (with humans inside) with alien faces, television aerials on their heads and television sets built into their rounded tummies. They speak a strange sort of baby-talk, mostly saying 'hello' ('eh-oh') and goodbye, and view the activities of human children on their own abdominal sets at odd intervals during their thirty-minute programme. Their appetite for Tubby toast and Tubby custard is insatiable. Quirky without being frighteningly odd, they are created for two- to four-year-olds with a few modest teaching aims built in. Some educators and parents have objected to their superficiality and wonder why toddlers should be watching television at all. But one thing is certain about the Teletubbies – they cannot be dubbed offensive on the grounds of over-sophistication or sexuality.[14]

Anne Wood herself was born in County Durham of a poor road-worker father. She was one of five children but the only child to reach adulthood. She looks back on her bleak childhood with a stoical lack of sentimentality, though she admits that John Lennon's 'Working Class Hero' is her favourite song. She declares that she is the product of the Education Act of 1944 in that she did well in secondary school, which for the first time was free to all. With top qualifications, she sailed into a good teaching job. As an English teacher at a secondary modern she became concerned that the children in her classes never appeared to read for pleasure. She succeeded in passing on the love of reading to her own two sons and in 1976 launched a magazine called *Books for Your Children* which won an award for national excellence. Yorkshire Television bought the rights to the magazine and turned it into a television programme. This was Wood's first contact with television.

She switched careers – from teaching and editing to producing children's television – in the eighties and was made head of Children's Programmes on TV-am, showing her flair for catching the public eye by giving Roland Rat his big breakfast spot in 1983. 'Everyone at TV-am was taking themselves so seriously, and I thought it would be fun to have a rat as a presenter,' she told an interviewer. Roland Rat was very successful in raising TV-am's flagging ratings in the summer of 1983, as already noted. But television bosses are not noted for their charitable impulses, and Bruce Gyngell fired Anne Wood when he took over as chief executive. She has the honesty to say she was deeply wounded by his decision to sack her; she is also able to smile now when she hears of Gyngell's amazement at the worldwide success of *Teletubbies*.

She has reason for satisfaction, for *Teletubbies* is watched by children of all ages in twenty-two languages and aired in forty-four countries. When she first created the 'fun-fur fab four', as one national newspaper dubbed them, with co-creator Andrew Davenport in 1994, she had minimal funds. To launch the series she had to take out a bank loan for her own company, Ragdoll Productions, and use the Tubbies as security. By 1998 she could look her bank manager square in the eye because she had the good sense to retain the US rights to the programme. A surge in licensing income from American merchandising meant that she made profits of £9 million on sales that year.

Anne Wood had successes before *Teletubbies*, and she had also generated audience disapproval. In 1984, after being fired by Gyngell, she launched a Channel 4 commission from Ragdoll called *Pob's Programme*. Pob, a bit of a punk doll, introduced each programme by spitting on screen and writing his name with his spit. This provoked enraged protests from some parents. In the manner that Anne Wood has developed over the years, she attempted to deflect their rage. Pob was only breathing on the glass, she said in his defence, and then using the moisture for writing.

In a similar manner, she defends her Teletubbies' behaviour against the cavils of critical educationists. Toddlers do talk baby-talk, she asserts, refuting accusations that their babble is idiotic. What is crucial to a pre-schooler's development, she insists, is watching and learning to move. Movement is basic to her teaching aims, and the Tubbies' way of walking, a sort of swaying propelled by rounded bottoms, does catch the essence of toddler motion.

Anne also wants to entertain toddlers. This is why she has a baby laughing in a nimbus of sunshine, why there are giant rabbits jumping about in their lunar landscape, why the cheerful voice (Eric Sykes's) can be heard from the mouth of a red horse and why the Tubbies, overcome by some obscure joy, are given to collapsing into each other's arms in endless hugs. She has already won a BAFTA award for entertaining pre-schoolers in other programmes, *Tots TV* and *Rosie and Jim*, and she has never been derivative (there not a hint of *Sesame Street*, for example, in her work). Her use of a vast green upland pasture for her Tubbies and their knowledge of technology (switching on their own abdominal sets and dealing with a Hoover called Noo Noo) are deliberate. 'They're going to be growing up in a technological world – why not get them used to it?' she asks.

She has been the target of a number of 'politically correct' critics as well as of professional educators. Many have pilloried her for being racist, as revealed by the lack of a black doll in her group of four. She counters by saying that the humans inside the Tubbies are multiracial – one is a Rastafarian, another a Cantonese woman. Anne Wood's responses are always soft, grandmotherly and unassailable. And that does not mean she is exploitable. When she began to feel that her *Tele-tubbies* income was being siphoned off by tortuous business contracts, she signed up for a self-help course in business finance.

Being misunderstood by sections of the public has not dented her confidence at all. The most astounding criticism to come her way – that the sweeping green pastureland which forms the Tubbies' playscape is a replica of a Nazi parade ground festooned with waving flags and even a bunker – was met with one of her now trademark pitying smiles. She had intended neither symbols of Gay Pride nor of neo-Nazism, she asserts emphatically. And she is never daunted. When the Tubbies' underground recreation centre, beneath the sixteen-foot-high Tubbytronic Superdome, became water-logged in the soggy Warwickshire farmland her team constructed a 200-yard drain to siphon off the water.[15]

While in no way mimicking Anne Wood's 'fab four', another highly successful programme dealing with four dolls skyrocketed to success in 1999. *The Tweenies* (BBC Worldwide) featured four ragdoll characters called Jake, Fizz, Milo and Bella. They are dressed, Tele-tubby-style, in bright colours of purple, blue, yellow and orange. They also have real people inside them to move their arms, legs and feet, but their heads are 'animatronic', rotated by remote control. BBC Worldwide chief executive Rupert Gavin defines *The Tweenies* as 'rock 'n' roll for children' because while the foursome chat and examine objects in their playroom they love to gyrate around in rhythmic dances, tapping their colourful sneakers as they twist and shake.

The Tweenies' creators are two actors in their forties, Iain Lauchlan and Will Brenton, who were relatively obscure pantomime dames until they dreamt up their foursome. (They were not new to children's television, however, having worked on *Playdays* in the eighties.) They heard through the media grapevine in the late nineties that the BBC was looking for a new pre-school programme to fill the age gap between *Teletubbies* and *Blue Peter*. 'We weren't invited to tender our ideas – we just gatecrashed and fired off an application form to the BBC anyway,' they told the *Daily Mirror* in January 2001.[16] Their idea was that it was time children watched replicas of themselves on television, not just fantasy dragons and dinosaurs. 'After all, as adults we like watching soaps, stories about ourselves. We thought it must be the same for pre-schoolers, that they'd like seeing their peers on screen.'

Though the BBC's executives insisted there would be no gender stereotyping of the characters, the two boys and two girls do act in girl–boy ways: Milo, the deep purple four-year-old boy, loves sport and kicking a ball around, while Fizz, aged four, and Bella, five, act in decidedly girlish ways, adoring ballet and pink accessories. Jake, a boy of two, behaves 'age-specifically', wearing nappies, crawling under things, emptying wardrobes and dismantling furniture in an evidently male toddler way.

The multiracial dimension is not emphasized in any glaring fashion, but Milo's spiky, corn-row hair is obviously African in style and Jake's punk quiff of bottle-blond hair speaks of a street-smart background. These are not middle-class children most at home on Pooh Corner. Their dog is a red mongrel called Doodles and the only human around is an ageing puppet called Max, dressed in an Alf Garnett cardigan (a grandparent figure?).

The programme aims to teach basic concepts such as space ('up and down'), size ('little and large') and matching ('red shoes with red dog') alongside the entertaining action and music. The Tweenies' catchphrase is 'Are you ready to play?' An edition of the programme that I watched on 15 November 1999 offered a brilliant exposition of the opposites 'up' and 'down'. Singing rhymes and dancing to a rocking salsa beat, the Tweenies went through a rich variety of ups and downs. Milo bounces up and down on a pogo stick; others send a balloon up and down. Fizz uses her dress-up butterfly wings to flap up and down, and Doodles, the dog, gets stuck up a tree and has to be brought down. To complete the 'up and down' theme, Milo goes up and down a slide in their townscape playground. I was impressed at how seamlessly the teaching and fun blended in this episode. Few children viewing it would experience anything but pleasure watching the jazzy foursome do what every child does: climbing, sliding, pogo-jumping. Yet at the same time the concept of up and down was being trenchantly explained. As Joan Ganz Cooney, *Sesame Street*'s creator, pointed out to me thirty years ago, conceptual thinking is one of the most difficult aspects of learning for a child, especially perhaps the urban child, where life is noisy, basic and often dismally confined.

With these two top-flight programmes, it looked by the end of the decade that the BBC was winning the competition in children's programming excellence and was out ahead in the lucrative merchandising race as well. *The Tweenies* brought in £25 million for BBC Worldwide in the first year of airing, and *Teletubbies* had accrued four times as much by 2000. Whenever commercial companies grumbled at this success, or disgruntled parents complained of being badgered by their children to buy spin-off toys from these shows, the BBC's executives had the perfect reply: 'We're keeping the TV licence down this way . . .'

Fortunately, ITV was not without its own success story in the nineties. *Art Attack*, an art show made by Media Merchants in Maidstone, Kent, and starring the presenter Neil Buchanan, first appeared in 1992 and is still going strong. Its spin-offs have included books (published by Dorling Kindersley and others) and art materials. It won a 1992 BAFTA award for 'Best Children's Factual Programme'. It is aimed at four- to sixteen-year-olds and intends to break down the idea that 'art is for eggheads – for the exceptional few' by showing that everyone can have fun with a pot of paint and a brush.

This was Neil Buchanan's vision – he has never had an art lesson in his life – but he was turned down by a handful of companies before striking gold with *Art Attack*. His huge success stems partly from the sheer physicality he puts into his art. A young, stylish presenter with chiselled good looks, he has all the electricity of a *Blue Peter* star, but he is doing much more than just chatting up the young viewers, gluing toilet rolls together and inviting his audience to support Guide Dogs for the Blind. His art creations are huge. In one show he used twenty black motor cars to make a picture of a bicycle (the cars were the wheels of the cycle). He is bold with his materials and rash with his subject matter. In a programme I watched in October 1999 he antici-pated upcoming Hallowe'en horrors by showing children how to make wounds, using red acrylic paint for blood, great lumps of wet Kleenex on top of plasters for livid gashes. Much of his popularity comes from his indifference to being 'nice'. His flair for monster montages is helped by the fact that he has a team of forty to help him in his Kent studio (the fact that he's a one-man phenomenon makes this surplus of help financially feasible).

He likes to be subtly educational. He will often teach children the difference between foregrounds and backgrounds, for example. In one sequence he painted a jungle scene (background) and then mounted cut-out cardboard boxes to jut out from the flat canvas. He was, in effect, creating a three-dimensional visual effect before young view-ers' eyes. And his frequent invitation to 'Try it yourself' is apparently enthusiastically followed.

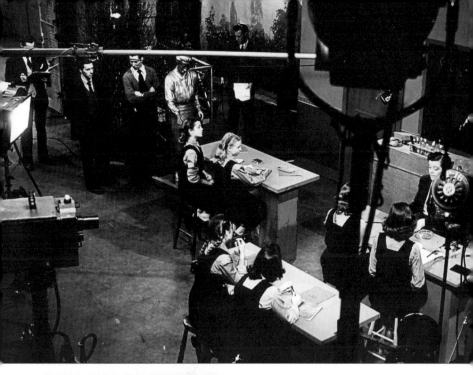

Above: Until the sixties children's programmes were made at Lime Grove Studios in London. Children of junior-school age were required by the Home Office to attend classes for a number of hours per week – when this picture was taken in 1952 the minimum number of hours was ten; it is now fifteen – hence this improvised classroom during Dorothea Brooking's reign as first head of children's drama.

Lord Reith, Director-General of the BBC at its inception in the fifties, seen here at a BBC drinks party with Dorothea Brooking, 1952

Andy Pandy and Teddy, created in the fifties by Freda Lingstrom for the BBC's *Watch With Mother* series. The programme was fairly unsophisticated (note the rather obvious strings on the puppets) but educational, a first for the under-fives.

Dorothea Brooking, acting as producer of *Meet the Penguins*, pictured here with the artist Bill Hooper in the fifties. This was one of the first animated model shows on television, predating *Trumpton* from the sixties.

Bill and Ben, the Flowerpot Men, with Little Weed. These three lived in terror of the Gardener, warning each other in Flobadob language of his approach, and producing glorious suspense for pre-school children. A new version of *Bill and Ben* was created in 2000 – minus strings.

The popularity and longevity of the BBC's *Blue Peter*, first transmitted in 1958, can be ascribed to the personalities of its presenters partly. Pictured from right to left are Peter Purves, Valerie Singleton and John Noakes who worked together in the late sixties and early seventies.

© BBC

Valerie Singleton in Hong Kong in the early seventies displays a *Blue Peter* badge and an oriental parasol. Awarding such badges to viewers helped to create a loyal fanbase and make them feel they were part of a club.

© BBC

The late Patrick Troughton became the second Dr Who in 1966 and played the role for three years. His expressive features and eccentric character in the part made him popular with viewers young and old.

© BBC

The fire brigade of the village of Trumpton assemble at the clocktower. Gordon Murray, the programme's creator in the sixties, says that this ideal village was probably somewhere in middle England.

© BBC

Thames Television became a serious rival to the BBC during the 1970s with its children's programmes. *Magpie*, in particular, challenged *Blue Peter* with its glamorous and trendy young presenters. Pictured here in 1972, from left to right, are Mick Robertson, Douglas Rae and Susan Stranks.

© Thames Television

Oliver Postgate with the famous cloth cat Bagpuss in the television studio in 1974. Postgate teamed up with Bagpuss's creator Peter Fermin at the beginning of the sixties, and they later went on to make *The Clangers* in a farm shed in Kent.

© BBC/Smallfilms

Dorothea Brooking taking a much-needed break
from rehearsing an adaption of Rumer Godden's
The Diddakoi, entitled *Kizzy*, at Lime Grove
Studios, filmed in 1976

Two of the BBC's most influential women in the field of children's television, Dorothea Brooking and Monica Sims (far right), appear at the Pye Colour Television Awards in 1980 for special services. Sims was head of BBC's Children's Programmes from 1967 to 1978. Brooking (at the microphone) was one of the BBC's first drama producers. Standing behind Sims is John Craven, of *Newsround* and *Play School* fame.

© BBC; reproduced by kind permission of Tim Brooking

Todd Carty (left) and Terry Siu Patt, the two rascally schoolboys who starred in *Grange Hill*, the popular seventies' and eighties' series, pictured in 1978. Carty went on to star in *Eastenders*.

© BBC

Commercial television scored a great hit with *Dangermouse*, which delighted audiences worldwide, gaining cult statues in the USA in the eighties on cable channel Nickelodeon. British television had traditionally imported American cartoon fare since the fifties, so this reverse trend was welcome. The programme, the brainchild of Mark Hall and Brian Cosgrove, was screened on Thames Television from 1981 to 1992.

The Wind in the Willows, based on Kenneth Grahame's magical tale, was another successful commercial television series in the eighties made by Mark Hall and Brian Cosgrove. A hundred technicians worked on the puppets, including model-makers, animators and cameramen.

© Cosgrove Hall/Thames Television

One of the best pre-school series to be made in Britain in the late nineties, *The Tweenies* is the creation of Iain Lauchlan and Will Brenton of Telltale Productions and features four Muppet-like unders-fives – Fizz, Bella, Milo and Jake – who subtly teach as they jive.

Barney, the purple dinosaur, sways, dances and smiles and teaches his friends, a group of pre-school children, about customs in other lands. An American creation, *Barney and Friends*, appears on Public Service Broadcasting in the USA and Channel Five in Britain.

Jeremy Swan, children's programme-maker, is shown directing *Sooty Heights* in 1999, starring the yellow bear (centre). This Sooty is a direct descendent of Harry Corbett's famous bear with black ears, the popular glove puppet of the fifties. Sooty, still going strong today, is an example of the successful updating of a fifty-year-old favourite.

A Kosovar child carries a comforting *Tellytubby* doll just before leaving on a plane trip home to his war-ravaged country. He was photographed in 1999 returning after a spell as a refugee in Britain.

© Press Association News/photographed by Owen Humphreys

Threading its way throughout the history of the BBC's children's programming has been the unspoken maxim 'If you've got a good formula, don't alter it.' Edward Barnes may have regretted the way *Grange Hill* plunged adolescents into the thick of issues such as pregnancy and contraception (or the lack of it), but when a new series was launched in early 2000 it was soon clear that *Grange Hill* had not become lily-livered or timorous as a result of the growls of the moral watchdogs in the early nineties. On the agenda were some tough subjects: newly divorced parents moping at home, women teachers and their 'toy-boys', soul-kissing ('It's slurpy, man!' declares one revolted teenager). Under the guidance of executive producer Elaine Sperber the programme maintained its record of unflinchingly reflecting the times.

The 23 January 2001 episode, for example, gave us pure Blairite Britain. The school is reflecting the pressure to achieve excellence and reveals the jockeyings for superiority among the visiting Ofsted (Office for Standards in Education) inspectors. 'Who are those old geezers?' asks one boy about a posse of businessmen passing him in the school hallway. 'They're redundant Ofsted workers,' replies a cheeky companion. When someone describes a pupil as 'different', another student offers the defence: 'He has six GCSEs – let's excuse him.' This is New Labour Britain 'on message'.

Another of the BBC's maxims could be 'Don't lose it, use it!' No children's programme is too old or creaky to be left mouldering in the archives. Nearly fifty years after their début in *Watch With Mother*, the string puppets Bill and Ben were pulled out of their storage drawers and revamped for a 21st-century comeback on 4 January 2001. Only this time there were no strings. After remodelling at Cosgrove Hall they seem freshly minted and well suited to their new animated form. They are moved by hand between each shot. The foam latex skin of the figure conceals an intricate metallic skeleton beneath. The work on the latex figures is laborious and painstaking, so much so that four

Cosgrove Hall animators produce no more than forty-eight seconds of film a day – an expensive undertaking. The characters still speak Flob-a-Dob language, but a star from *Cold Feet,* John Thomson, provides the voices of the flowerpot men. Some appealing new animated garden creatures have been added to the repertoire to engage pre-schoolers: Pry the Magpie, Scamper the Squirrel, Tad the Frog and Boo the Hedgehog.

People are very sensitive to changes made to their favourite childhood programmes, I've found. *Evening Standard* television critic Victor Lewis-Smith, who confesses that *Watch With Mother* was the highlight of his day as a five-year-old, has mourned the modernity of the new Bill and Ben, writing: 'My first reaction was that the flowerpot men must have emigrated to some forgotten corner of Tellytubbyland, such is the garishness of the garden they now inhabit.'[17] Present-day television animators perhaps forget how tenacious a factor nostalgia can be for many people. Seeing Bill and Ben in bright colours could be quite a shock – rather like seeing Harry Lime in Berlin in a Hawaiian shirt.

However, Jeremy Swan, veteran children's television programme-maker, had no qualms about revamping *Sooty* for the BBC when I met him soon after he had completed thirteen episodes of *Sooty Heights*, a kind of *Fawlty Towers* for bears. Sooty was bright yellow in his new incarnation, very different from his erstwhile monochromatic appearance on Harry Corbett's piano nearly fifty years ago. 'I've changed Sooty quite a bit for *Sooty Heights*,' Swan acknowledged. 'Because he was small and cuddly, he could be pretty anarchic in the past. He used to squirt people with a water pistol. The watchdog monitors were very wary of that pistol.'

He has fourteen nieces and nephews living in his native Ireland and often runs ideas for episodes by them. He thinks *double entendre* is inappropriate for children. 'When in doubt, cut it out, is my maxim,' he says. 'As a producer of children's television you have to keep a measure of decorum. I would never put something in an episode that a mother would have to explain. When Sooty and his chums were baking buns for tea in *Sooty Heights*, we toyed with the idea of mentioning there was a bun in the oven and then threw it out. We excised the whole thing. No oven, no lemon juice on loo paper. You really can't force adult jokes down children's throats, sort of talk down to them. It just isn't on.'

Jeremy Swan may be right about leaving adult humour to adults, but in the past some successful so-called children's programmes did go in for shadowy grown-up references, and no one appeared to be harmed. As already mentioned, *The Magic Roundabout* often seemed to make reference to the prevailing drug culture in the mid-sixties, but pre-schoolers would not have noticed. Lovers of the show cannot get enough of it, in any case. A Bristol company, the Bolexbrothers, is in the process of making a film version of *The Magic Roundabout*, scheduled to appear in 2003. It will include all the original Serge Danot characters: Dougal the dog, Ermintrude the cow, Brian the snail, Dylan the rabbit and Zebidee. Andy Leighton, managing director of Bolexbrothers, says that the company will preserve the original but develop the characters to satisfy all ages.

Not everyone is happy about these remakes and revamps of thirty- and forty-year-old programmes such as *The Flowerpot Men* and *The Magic Roundabout*. A *Daily Telegraph* critic wrote on 19 February 2000: 'Do we look forward to wallowing in nostalgia as we sit beside our children? No, we do not . . . It is sad that these children's programme-makers with millions to spend and all day to dream up ideas, end up raking through old filing cabinets.' Indeed, given the excellence and originality of current programme-making in Britain for the under-tens, it is doubtful whether we need so much excavation.

British television for the under-tens tends to be squeaky clean, unlike US cartoon serials for the family such as *South Park* and *The Simpsons*, which are brilliant but shot through with adult sophistication, regardless of whether it is understood by the young or not.

There is certainly no trace of smut in *Bob the Builder*, an animation series first broadcast by the BBC in 1999, featuring the voice of actor Neil Morrissey from the *Men Behaving Badly* sitcom, both chanting and speaking. *Bob* is the BBC's latest 'outreach commission' success. Moon-faced Bob and his yellow hard-hat take us back to the Trumptonshire of the sixties; like his predecessors he takes pride in his job. His catchphrase is 'Can we fix it?' to which he himself replies, 'Yes, we can!' He is helped by some friendly machines who make iron and steel sound positively cosy: Muck the bulldozer, Lofty the crane, Roley the steamroller and Dizzy the cement mixer.

Bob could be called 'son of *Sesame Street*' because many of the programme's makers were once assistants to the late, great Jim Henson when he was making Muppets in Britain in the eighties. Peter Orton, founder of the company that owns *Bob*, HIT Entertainments, worked for Henson as advertising art director. When he went home to his three young children he told them bedtime stories of his own invention which centred on a building site digger that later became Scoop. He then created Bob along with his other mechanical sidekicks. He sent out the story to dozens of possible directors and accumulated a mountain of rejection slips over the years.

Bob deserves his belated success. He is the quintessential optimist, and there is undoubtedly something very comforting about a stalwart young man who can 'fix' things. His customers in the rural never-never-land he inhabits speak in clear, good English, free of any attempt at any local dialect or currently trendy Estuary English. The series is produced in two run-down warehouses in Altrincham, Cheshire, called Hothouse Animation. The company's managing director, Jackie Cockle, is a former Cosgrove Hall animator. The world of children's animation is indeed a tight, almost incestuous one.

The show got its biggest boost when Bob's Christmas song made it to No. 1 in the charts over Christmas 2000, outselling even Rap singer Eminem – notorious for his lugubrious songs about chain-sawing hap-

less females in two. To many appalled parents, Bob's victory repre-
sented the triumph of innocence over evil (though his success
probably sprang largely from its popularity among chanting football
fans). Whatever the reasons, *Bob the Builder* raked in £60 million in
tie-in merchandising within six months of its launch.

Overall, the nineties proved to be a satisfying decade for children's
television. In Britain the 'outsourcing' edict seems to have tapped into
some extraordinary talent: small, fecund studios producing charm and
near genius from uninspiring huts and warehouses in obscure locales
of provincial England. US critics noticed a change for the better in the
nineties, too: grotesques like the *Ninja Turtles* and *Power Rangers* were
still screened, but there were no new imitations. And American
watchdogs were pleased with at least one new cartoon addition – Barney, the six-foot purplish-blue dinosaur with a soft heart. The
celebrations were muted, however. As Kate Taylor, Director of
Boston's Channel 2 Children's Programmes, put it in 1998: 'The danger is we become satisfied because it is so much better overall. It
couldn't have gotten much worse, when you look at where we were
five years ago, with one show after another that was toy-based, violent,
simplistic. There was no place to go but up.'[18]

In Lord Reith's day in the fifties, the view that had greatest sway at
the BBC was that children should have a 'protected' area, a sacrosanct
slot of their own. The truth is, however, that the nation's children
themselves apparently did not want to be herded gently into 'made for
children' paddocks. Both children and their parents were most
strongly drawn to light entertainment, it appeared. Robert Silvey, the
BBC's head of Research, wrote at the time, drawing on the findings
of his Audience Research Department in the early fifties: 'A startling
two-thirds of 7–11s claimed to like "cabaret" very much, and the
12–14s stood out as the group with the highest proportion of enthusi-
asts for cabaret, sports outside broadcasts, newsreels and feature
films.'[19]

This came as no surprise to the child experts of the time, the most impressive of whom was Dr Hilde Himmelweit, who commented in 1958:

> From the findings presented so far, we have learned four things about the children's tastes. Firstly, they were so varied that even the most favoured programmes received only 30 per cent of the votes. Second, from the age of 10 (and we suspect even earlier) children preferred adult programmes to those specifically designed for them. Third, children with access to both channels more often watched ITV rather than BBC. Fourth, that supply affected taste; it lies, to some measure, within the power of television to broaden our narrow children's taste, to make it more, or less, mature.[20]

This rather embarrassing array of findings forced the BBC to drop the generic term 'children's television' for a short period in the fifties. ITV, which had tended to be less concerned about the child/adult distinction in the first place, carried on as usual, interspersing its Westerns and adventure dramas (such as *Robin Hood*) with the usual cartoon fare, the latter largely imported from the USA. Fathers, most of them just back from work in the early evenings, watched the teatime fare through glazed eyes, and mothers, close to hearth and stove in those days, were also distracted. So from 4 to 6 p.m. young teenagers were the most intent consumers of light entertainment.

By the nineties, however, the adult/child distinction had become almost completely blurred, and combined adult–child viewing, sometimes called 'kidult' viewing, had become a permanent feature of evening television in Britain. That superb animated cartoon *The Simpsons* (shown on BBC 2 and Sky One, usually between 6 and 7 p.m.) transfixed parents and children alike, seated shoulder to shoulder before the flickering screen. This worried some child experts, who were concerned that the show's many political allusions and sexual innuendoes might corrupt or mystify children.

They need not have been so perturbed. Adults and children have been sharing entertainments for centuries. An example is the Christmas pantomime, which emerged in Britain during the seventeenth century. Panto developed out of the Renaissance Commedia dell'Arte, in which street performers and small theatrical troupes converged to produce spontaneous theatre, improvising language and plots as they went along. Like its predecessor, panto revelled in improvisation and theatrical panache, mixing tongue-in-cheek bravura and exuberant irreverence. It is delightfully formulaic. There is always a villain, a principal boy, a 'dame' (frequently an ugly man in drag), a 'cheeky chappie' who is normally besotted (hopelessly) with the incredibly sweet, altruistic and gullible heroine. Both adults and children boo the villain and shout warnings to the hapless principal boy and beautiful girl: 'Look out, he's *behind* you . . . !' Gender-bending abounds, and one of the saucy aspects of the show is that the principal boy (a woman) and heroine fall in love – a naughtily Sapphic touch.

Embedded in this figurative Christmas pudding of a drama is the ever-present risqué *double entendre*.

Villain: There's something very attractive about you, but I can't quite put my finger on it . . .

Dame: No and you ain't going to, either![21]

The parents and children in the audience are all convulsed with laughter. But do the five-year-olds really get it? I doubt it. Does it matter? I cannot think that it does. Children are not corrupted by lines like these, but they can become disastrously over-excited. I saw a child at the Hackney Empire's production of *Mother Goose* in January 2001 lying in the aisle having a monster tantrum at intermission time, drumming his little feet on the floor and howling while his ice lolly dribbled over his short pants. Try explaining the reason for an inter-mission to a tired five-year-old who has been screaming 'He's *behind* you!' repeatedly for forty-five minutes.

Himmelweit and other researchers show that 'kidult' viewing existed well before the nineties. *The Flintstones* had blazed the trail in the sixties. Cosgrove Hall's *Dangermouse*, first shown in 1981, further developed the habit of family viewing. Adults developed a passion for Secret Agent Mouse and his bumbling hamster assistant, Penfold, partly because of the clever scripts and partly because of their James Bond-style cars and gadgetry (Dangermouse drives a low-slung beauty of a white saloon car). Children liked the slapstick and enjoyed the cool verbal asides voiced by actor David Jason. And when a cartoon captures both age groups the makers are on to a possible fortune. During its life span *Dangermouse* amassed 6 million viewers at home and abroad and was screened in thirty-one countries. There was also a wide variety of spin-off merchandise – three videos, books, coffee mugs, maps and, oddly, Wellington boots.[22]

The fact that families like watching other families on screen has led some television analysts to suggest that the sight of a group of happy parents and children enjoying a barbecue or a neighbourhood party together, as they often did in *The Flintstones*, gives reflected plea-sure to family viewers (though, as some pessimists point out, cartoon characters are being a great deal more active than their viewers). My own guess is that viewing programmes together probably does help family cohesiveness but in ways that are beneath the surface and quite subtle. Part of the pleasure for the child is in wondering what part of the dialogue or action is tickling their father's or mother's fancy and why. Parents' private estimates of events always interest their children, at least in their younger years. When they reach fourteen or fifteen children lose interest in their parents' views and reactions, but in what child psychiatrists call the latency period (around ten to twelve years) the young are especially interested in their parents' inner thoughts, unbidden laughter and quick, unexpected chortles. It is not unusual to see a child's head swinging from parent to screen and back again as though they are watching a tennis match. Sometimes they cannot resist asking: 'So what's so funny about that?'

The Simpsons, the last word in 'kidult' viewing worldwide, had a strange genesis. Matt Groening, its American creator, was a none-too-successful Los Angeles-based cartoon animator when he was asked to create a 'bumper' – a sort of cartoon filler – for the struggling *Tracey Ullman Show* in 1987. Groening submitted his surreal family saga, based in the suburban town of Springfield, admitting that he had drawn on his own family for the names of the principal characters – Homer, Madge (the parents) and Bart, Lisa and baby Maggie (the off-spring). Bart – an anagram of 'brat' – is an endearing but stupid child of ten who is constantly getting into trouble; Lisa is a gifted eight-year-old, and a faintly moralistic little girl; Maggie just sucks on her plastic dummy. Homer is a lazy and cowardly blue-collar, beer-drinking chump with a large belly curling over the top of his trousers. Madge, with her blue cone of hair, is tolerant, amorous and permissive, alternately babying and nagging Homer and being a concerned mother when she can tear herself away from 'good works': striving for inter-racial harmony, the triumph of feminism and exposure of the shenanigans of corrupt local politicians (one lecherous politico in Springfield's local government bears an uncanny resemblance to John F. Kennedy).

The Simpsons, visually a very orange-yellow cartoon with splashes of blue (Madge's hair, for instance), plays on a sort of Russian doll effect: we're watching television and watching the Simpsons watch it, too. Their comments on other television programmes can be cutting and satirical. When watching *60 Minutes*, America's answer to *Panorama*, Homer remarks with satisfaction: 'Ah, television – teacher, mother, secret lover!' He is not often so thoughtful, although he has achieved a sort of literary fame now that his ejaculation 'Doh!' has entered the *Oxford English Dictionary* as an expression of injury or disgust. His favourite hang-out, Moe's Tavern, is a hotbed of substance abuse presided over by the proprietor, belching Barney. Homer is addicted to beer and doughnuts, which he consumes as he sprawls flat out on his living-room couch. His pet hate is neighbour Ned Flanders, a mewling, unquestioning Christian fundamentalist given to uttering Sibylline remarks about the 'all-important unknowns' of life. He is, in Homer's view (when he's sober enough to formulate a view), a total nerd. The town of Springfield is a hymn to the dysfunctional relationship.

Groening's left-wing liberal politics are very apparent in the show and so irked former President George Bush that he made the memorable comment in 1992: 'Let's have American families be closer to the Waltons than the Simpsons.' (The Waltons were a saccharine Midwestern family, popular in the eighties.) Fox Studios, which first aired *The Simpsons* in 1990 and continues to do so, could not have had better publicity if they had rented all the billboards that proclaim their messages beside highways across the USA.

The show's popularity was also boosted by celebrity guest appearances doing voice-overs. More importantly, people were getting a bit tired of the prevailing 'political correctness', and Groening tapped into this undercurrent of *ennui*. *The Simpsons* carried all before it, with its comically subversive messages – not just in the USA but across the globe. In the year 2000 it was voted one of the most popular television programmes in British television history. The *Tracey Ullman Show* had meanwhile died a death . . .

I recently interviewed a mother and her teenage son who live in Epping, Essex, to discover what draws them to *The Simpsons*. Tracy Gardiner, thirty-eight, who works as a research executive for an Essex medical company, had raised her son, fifteen-year-old John, as a single parent since he was a toddler. He is now a towering, six-foot-tall secondary schoolboy who plays football more avidly than he watches television and is soon to take his mock GCSEs. John and Tracy are a close mother–son duo, but they give each other considerable space for individual pursuits. Tracy's recent second marriage and new motherhood have not greatly disturbed this comfortable relationship. A few weeks before our interview Tracy had broken her leg on a skiing trip, so she was watching more television than usual. She and John had just started watching *The Simpsons* together. They spoke about their combined viewing:

Tracy: John and I have never watched TV together before now, but we've become recently hooked on *The Simpsons*. I love it. It's funny and yet moralistic at the same time.

John: Little kids learn a lesson from it, even though I do think it has a low laughter rate.

Tracy: All groups find it funny. I'm not sure I agree with John about the low laughter rate, but I agree it's instructive. I'm intrigued to see how Madge struggles to raise her children. It's so ordinary, so life-like.

John: It's full of messages. Remember when Homer tried to put on fake hair so he wouldn't look so bald when he went for a job at the Springfield town nuclear plant? Well, his kids sort of comforted him and told him he shouldn't worry about not having hair. It's about normal family life.

Tracy: The show is prime-time TV, and there's something for all age groups. It's brilliant that a cartoon series can reach so many differing types of viewers. It's not really a comedy, either. I mean John and I aren't cracking ourselves up laughing. It gives us more of a smile.

139

John: I like Abe the granddad and the way you see Bart manipulating him for ice cream and so on. And I think it's great that Homer is lazy and drinks masses of beer. I don't disapprove of him. I accept that that's just the way he is.

The Simpsons pleases intelligent young teenagers like John and it also has sages and university dons pondering its values. In one serious analysis of its significance published on an American educational website, the show receives some extravagant intellectual praise. In an article called 'Yellow trash', academic Alex Lesman writes:

Perhaps *The Simpsons*, premièring at the end of a decade of Republican presidents and wholesome sitcoms like *The Cosby Show*, appeared at just the right time to satisfy a national hunger for something saltier. . . . The corruption and decay of the Simpsons' era relative to that of the Waltons is debatable, but many contemporary viewers seem to recognize and accept the Simpsons' moral decay . . . still, despite that slight bias, the show is never crudely orthodox. Institutions that are traditionally associated with the left, like organized labor, are also subject to ridicule, though not as often as those associated with the right, like big business . . . Yet traditionally liberal concerns, such as tight funding for public schools, high-priced medical care and huge military budgets, are frequently presented as problems.[23]

Matt Groening himself puts the show's purpose more succinctly: 'There is an ongoing subtext to *The Simpsons*, and that is that the people in power don't always have your best interests at heart.'

Whatever the cartoon's radical meanings, it has perhaps ironically become a huge commercial success. An advertising campaign featuring Bart Simpson sold Butterfinger bars (a chocolate and molasses sweet sold in the USA) in 1993, helping Nestlé to increase its sales by

51 per cent. By February 1994, four years after its television début, $100 million worth of Simpsons merchandise licences had been sold.

Another animated cartoon series brought to life in the nineties, *South Park*, has become a serious rival to *The Simpsons* in the combined viewing stakes. While both shows are crammed with political in-jokes, *The Simpsons* is more straightforwardly humorous, fairly free of scatological baggage and serious social commentary. Its script takes aim at a few sacred cows, of course – feminism, religious moralism and windy politicians among them. But *South Park* is altogether more savage and plunges into subjects that make most of us wince merely to contemplate, such as anti-Semitism, euthanasia and incurable illness. But, for all its outrageousness, it is also hugely popular with both parents and children. The difference between the two shows is perhaps that with *The Simpsons* parents do not usually mind if their children get the point of the jokes, while with *South Park* they smile, gaze heavenwards and pray that they don't.

Sweet as its cartoon figures appear, *South Park* is a ride on the wild side for children. Its content, scrutinized carefully, is about as suitable for the young as the mad ramblings of the Marquis de Sade – death, anal obsessiveness and incontinence are its stock-in-trade. Personally, I feel it is cheating deliberately to wing over your immature viewers' heads, but maybe the huggable quality of its four main boy characters is enough of a smokescreen to prevent undue worry about the endless scatology (farting contests and so on) and smirking glances at the fall-out created for women by the menopause.

South Park is aired after the nine o'clock watershed (on Channel 4 at 9.30 p.m. in Britain; at 10 p.m. on Comedy Central in the USA), so the television companies cannot be accused of brandishing unsuitable material at the under-twelves before bedtime. For a change, the blame – if there is any blame involved – can be placed solidly with the parents if the material disturbs some children.

South Park started life with the intention of shocking viewers, and it continues to do so. It began as a five-minute animated film made by Trey Parker and Matt Stone, two young men from Colorado. It was originally created as a short film 'Christmas Card' for a Fox network executive in 1995. It was entitled 'The Spirit of Christmas' and featured the four now familiar third-grade schoolboys witnessing an obscene martial arts battle between Jesus and Santa Claus. It became an underground success almost immediately. Trey and Parker then amplified this short one-off work, eventually parlaying it into the present half-hour series.

The four schoolboys who star in *South Park* are Stan Marsh, aged eight, who has a 102-year-old grandfather who wants to die; Kyle Broslovsky, Stan's Jewish friend, who is sensitive to the fact that he practises a different religion from his chums and is also embarrassed by his mother's noisily expressed premenstrual stress disorders; Eric Cartman, a fat kid who claims to be 'big-boned' but who devours doughnuts; and Kenny, who is short for his age, wears a hooded jacket which muffles his voice, and dies during each episode. And there are some other marvellous characters, among them Mr Garrison, the boys' teacher, who badly needs anger management training; Chef, the school cook who sings sexually explicit songs over the frying pan; Stan's uncle, Uncle Jimbo, who owns the local gun shop; and Wendy Testaburger, the bright girl of eight who fires Stan's love interest. The major catchphrase from the series occurs each week after Kenny dies: 'Oh my God! They killed Kenny!'

(Incidentally, Kenny's demise does not seem to worry most children. Emmie Giles, a nine-year-old from Exeter, Devon, wrote me: 'I don't mind it when Kenny dies. I know he's going to be alive again next week.' Emmie watches *South Park* with her two teenage brothers; 'combined viewing' can also refer to older siblings, of course.)

The death and the scatology – one of the foursome is not potty-trained, a problem made visible with a brown stain – are perhaps tempered by the cuteness of the round-faced offenders. *South Park* employs an unusual animated technique using figures made of thick cardboard. This technique is cheap: each episode of *South Park* costs 75 per cent less to produce than a similar *Simpsons* slot, for example.

The *double entendre* is sometimes almost too obscure for a sophisticated Chelsea raver or Manhattan sex chick. For example, I watched a Hallowe'en sequence on 30 October 1999 in which one of the group entreats the gang to play the traditional American Hallowe'en game of 'Bobbing for Apples'. This game, as many probably know, involves leaning over a barrel of apples floating in water and trying to lift one free with one's mouth and teeth. 'Come on, let's bob for apples,' says the MC on the programme. 'Yes, come on, girls, use some of those mouth muscles Peking girls are famous for.' I guess this was an obscure reference to the expertise of Chinese prostitutes at the practice of fellatio and also a hint at current tittle-tattle about a similar skill supposedly learnt by the Duchess of Windsor in the Far East. Murky, or what? But this kind of in-joke creates a sense of cohesion among the script-writers on set and adds to the fun of working in a small film company; it is also reminiscent of *Private Eye* under Richard Ingrams's editorship in the seventies and eighties.

The world of animated cartoons certainly is pretty incestuous, as we noticed in connection with Cosgrove Hall and the companies formed by its former employees in Britain. In the USA another 'kidult' favourite of the nineties, *The Rugrats*, sprang directly from the studio of Matt Groening, creator of *The Simpsons*. Three animators who met on the set of *The Simpsons* in 1988 were a married couple, Arlene Klasky and Gabor Csupo, plus Paul Germain. All three were new parents, swamped by nappies and the daily rigours of toilet training. They conceived the notion of creating a series that would show the world from a baby's point of view. *The Rugrats* was first broadcast on Nickelodeon in 1990 with sixty-five episodes. Two films have subsequently been made, the second (*Rugrats in Paris*) in 2001, featuring the marvellous voice of actress Susan Sarandon as a child-hating Frenchwoman.

The show centres on the activities of a group of babies and toddlers led by Tommy Pickles, two-year-old Chuckie, who is afraid of clowns, eighteen-month-old twins Phil and Lil Deville, Tommy's parents and grandparents, both paternal and maternal, and Spike the dog. The babies have big pale bobbing heads crowned by scraggy tufts of hair, T-shirted chests and bare feet. Tommy's leadership is marked by his wearing of a colonial pith helmet which he sometimes has difficulty keeping on his head when his nappies sag and need hitching. He and his obedient gang are often trapped in forests and pursued by ghoulies and ghosties, but his trusty screwdriver lends them as much comfort as a Viking clansman's broadsword.

There is an undertow of morality: Tommy Pickles never forgets to protect his baby brother, Dylan, who cries all the time. At the same time there is the usual smutty talk that seems to thread its way through all of these West Coast successes of the nineties. For example, Lil, one of the twins, joins the group in jumping on a mattress in the first Rugrats film (*The Rugrats Movie*, 1998). Jumping for joy in mid-air, she trills: 'This is more fun that picking noses!' There is much noisy baby agreement and the addition of the solemnly voiced conviction that farting is also a great game.

I have to confess that I take limited pleasure in this series. Indeed, much of the babies' conversation strikes me as being positively gnomic. However, my bright ten-year-old granddaughter Phoebe finds it hilarious, especially its catchphrase: 'Hang on to your diapies . . .' So who am I to complain? It also seems a bit churlish not to have as much fun watching the show as its creators evidently have making it. Composer Mark Mothersbaugh writes about the atmosphere in the Los Angeles studio where the programme is produced:

> One of the qualities of Klasky Csupo is they are a really healthy hotbed of organized chaos. I remember all these people coming over when we were working on the theme song for the TV series.

They all had different ideas on how to go with the music and it was kind of like, 'Wow, this is wild.' Everybody forged opinions about everything even if it wasn't their area of expertise. That's kind of how it works over there. People that are working in inking or painting can offer suggestions to people in sound design, and people that are working on the music can offer suggestions to the story writers.[24]

Not that animation is always about joyous group play. Nick Park, the creator of *Wallace and Gromit*, winner of both BAFTA and Oscar awards, is more sober about the process. Director of Aardman Animations, Bristol, he is too meticulous to churn out endless episodes in the life of the soppy inventor and his pointy-eared dog.

One of Park's best-known short films, *The Wrong Trousers*, was first broadcast in 1994, part-sponsored by the BBC, and has been shown many times since. Like his other productions, the film is delightful and its appeal broad and enduring, but making them is *hard work*, he insists. Wallace and Gromit are made of Plasticine, and making them appear to be talking and smiling using this material is a finicky business. Park prefers to employ a small group of animators instead of the teams favoured in California. He often has no more than seven animators working at the same time, and says that an animator normally ompletes only two to three seconds of screen time a day.

Park was born in Preston, Lancashire, and draws on his childhood memories for many of his plots. His father was the model for the bulbous-nosed, goggle-eyed Wallace, for he spent most of his leisure time in the garden shed making weird contraptions when Park was growing up.

Wallace and Gromit are usually classified as 'family entertainment', but Park does not like his precious duo to be pigeonholed into any particular category. When asked if he saw his films as being for children, he replied: 'No, not all – nor adults really. I don't think of either audience but I think of myself as it! So I suppose in that sense I am making the films for myself. I think of an audience full of me!'[25]

This remark intrigues me because it reinforces my conviction that people who make films or write books or cartoon series for children have a strong sense of their 'inner child', that slightly arch psychiatric phrase. The best children's presenters also seem to have the ability to make contact with the feelings they had as children, along with a fairly calm temperament. The qualities of being human and *simpatico* shone through in Mr Rogers, who soothed and delighted the whole family in sixties' America and again in the charming and relaxed actor Bill Cosby, star of *The Cosby Show.* These men are quiet, apparently thoughtful and do not scream, shout or gesticulate at their viewers.

Rolf Harris is the current winner in the 'family audience' presenter stakes on this side of the Atlantic. Rolf shows genuine sympathy for both animals and their troubled owners in BBC 1's *Animal Hospital* and is quite captivating. Though *Animal Hospital*, which began life in the late nineties, is not strictly regarded as a children's programme, it has a pre-watershed slot (usually 8 or 8.30 p.m.) so children can and do watch it in large numbers. And its compassion for animals follows in a long BBC tradition beginning with *Blue Peter* over forty years ago.

Cold-calling celebrities was one of my least favourite activities when I worked for the *Daily Express* in the eighties, but Rolf Harris made it a pleasure. At the time he was enchanting child audiences in a BBC *Children's Hour* show where, as Anna Home puts it, he operated a kind of 'animated easel', drawing cartoons as they appeared to pop into his mind.[26] He was very modest about his talent as a cartoonist. 'I go into a sort of trance,' he said. 'I've never had any training. I can hardly explain how it all comes about . . . it's a sort of happening.' And he had been making it happen since the fifties when he joined a BBC children's magazine show called *Whirligig* which was broadcast from 1952 to 1956.

Thinking of the dozens of children's programme-makers and entertainers I have met over the years, I would say they are blessed with more modesty than the 'for adults' variety of presenter. There is less ego and more altruism about them. John Coop, the gentle giant head of Granada's Children's Department in the sixties and seventies, was so unassuming and pleasant when I found him sitting on top of a desk in producer Pauline Shaw's office that I thought he couldn't have been an executive. Those were the days of tough-talking, 'effing and blinding' director/producers like Tim Hewat and Bill Grundy, who had machismo and peacock vanity etched into their personae, brilliant and talented as they were in their way. Bill Grundy, predominantly an 'adult' presenter, could recall only one childhood experience, as I look back on our many conversations, and that was of his tough, working-class Mancunian mother letting him eat the white tops of her breakfast boiled eggs when he was six. In contrast, Jeremy Swan, Sooty's present master, has a treasure-trove of memories and delves into them every time he returns to Ireland to see his fourteen nieces and nephews.

I met children's presenter Leslie Crowther in 1990, just before the tragic automobile accident that shortened his life. Having not long before seen a repeat of his *Flanagan and Allen* drama-documentary, I expected the worldliness of a Chesney Allen (the 'smoothie' of the famous music-hall duo which he enacted, but in fact he was direct, simple, warm and approachable. He was much more like the BBC's *Crackerjack!* host that he had been in the early sixties. He had gar-nered a wealth of experience after many years as a comic performer and after-dinner speaker, but what mattered to him much more was the fact that he could see Lord's cricket ground from the window of his London flat. 'I was a passionate cricketer as a kid,' he told me, his eyes shining. 'In my wildest, I could never have visualized owning a flat

147

right over the famous grounds. Every time I look out over the pitch, I have to pinch myself. How lucky can you get?'

Crowther was deeply involved in charity work, and this seems to be another common feature of child presenters. One has only to think of *Tiswas*'s Lenny Henry (shown on ATV in the seventies) and his remarkable work over the years for Comic Relief. It seems a natural corollary that entertaining children also makes the entertainer want to help those who are disadvantaged.

In *The Quest for the Big Woof*,[27] a collection of random thoughts and cartoons, Lenny Henry writes of the people who have most influenced him: Jerry Lewis, Abbot and Costello, Joan Rivers, Bob Hope, Tracey Ullman, Jack Benny, Mel Brooks, Bill Cosby. He notes that they are educated people and then adds: 'Maybe things would be easier if I had some . . . QUALIFICATIONS!' And then answers himself: 'But NAAH, I was too busy at school looking out of the window.' Judging from the excellence of his recent portrayal of a headmaster in the BBC's *Hope and Glory*, he was not as much of an air-head as he suggests. But somehow I don't think he curled up with the philosophical musings of Kant and Descartes, either. And in this too he resembles many other presenters of children's programmes.

Child presenters are often famous, but they seldom need body-guards to control the press of fans. I once interviewed Bernard Cribbins for a column I was writing for *Queen* magazine. He was the star presenter of the illustrious BBC *Jackanory* series in the swinging sixties, but there was nothing particularly swinging about him. Dressed solemnly in tweeds, he toyed with his coffee at the Piccadilly Hotel table where we sat and confessed he had no idea at all why children liked listening to him. He appeared, if anything, more nervous about our interview than I was. Nobody recognized him, not even the waiter. And in the eighties Floella Benjamin, at the time famous for her appearances on the BBC children's show *Fast Forward* and author of a successful book of corny jokes for children, told me: 'Oh, sometimes the Jamaican grannies where I live in south-east London will look at me open-mouthed, wave their arms around and say, "There is she!" But they don't crowd in on me, and I think they're sweet.' She appreciated not having her privacy invaded as intrusively as other television celebrities have come to expect.

All in all, Noel Coward might have added to his warning to Mrs Worthington not to put her daughter on the stage that she might consider training her to be a children's presenter. She would probably have a quieter life.

6

From Bagpuss to Big Business

Children and Merchandising

'Peter and I pushed ideas backwards and forwards for quite a long time. The cat, whose name, we concluded, was Bagpuss, was English, certainly retired, and sedentary, preferring to sleep on his own cushion. All cats, given the opportunity, will choose to sleep in a shop window where it is warm and they can be admired without being disturbed.' – Oliver Postgate[1]

The mention of shop windows brings us to the topic of marketing products to small children. Oliver Postgate, who never received anything like full credit for his pioneering role in children's television, once defined merchandising as 'the selling of consumer products so as to connect them with television characters. Today it is an enormous industry.'[2] And so is the related phenomenon of licensing. Merchandising deals occur when a 'studio licenses to a manufacturer the right to use names, characters and artwork for spin-off products such as toys, clothing, novelizations and soundtrack albums'.[3] More specifically, character licensing is an agreement that grants the right to use a name or image in exchange for a royalty fee (generally 5–15 per cent of the wholesale cost of an item).[4]

In its simplest form, 'merchandising' is what happens when a beloved television programme or character is converted from one medium into another. During the marketing process there are shifts in the balance of power between children, their parents and manufacturers or advertisers – often with surprising consequences.

Let us begin with the most fundamental question. Why do children love toys so much? And why does this mean that commerce can manipulate them? One leading authority offered the following explanation. According to child psychologist Lewis P. Lipsitt, founder of Brown University's Child Study Center, toys 'are props in rehearsing behavior, and building blocks for fantasy, in turn the foundation for creativity and self-expression. Toys are to a kid what a hammer is to a carpenter – they enhance his ability to build things.'[5]

Toys also appeal to the desire to collect (more a question of 'accumulating stuff' in the case of very young children); marketing campaigns are often designed with that hunter-gatherer impulse in mind. Toys may elicit latent managerial tendencies in the child, besides opening up a secret inner world in which parents play no part. Toys and other collectables may be infused with subjective mystical significance. Indeed, there may be some parallel with religious relics. Toy-collecting also confers a sort of power to children: a toy Dalek (such as the one from 1966 on display at the Science Museum in London) is vastly more malleable and less threatening than a real alien robot would be.

Children have complex relationships with their toys. Sometimes they identify with them but not always. Dan Acuff has described a phenomenon he calls 'disidentification', which is 'a different type of identification, in which the child does *not* want to be like a human or animal character but is attracted to and involved with it because of its "dark side". (Villains are typical objects of disidentification, e.g. Darth Vader in *Star Wars* . . . or "soft" villains such as Wile E. Coyote in *Road Runner*.)'[6]

To review the toy industry's activities over the twentieth century is to unearth a cultural history in miniature: toy campaigns are a barometer of changing social and cultural mores. The 19 October 1995 *Wall Street Journal* recounted a 1917 advertisement for Daisy Air Rifles ('It's a natural instinct for every American boy to want a gun'). Later, Mickey Mouse toys provided friendship and comfort to young people during the testing times of the Depression (at $4.95 each, which was a substantial sum in those days).[7] 'Shirley Temple' dolls soon followed. In 1954–5 coonskin caps from Disney's Davy Crockett became a huge national fad across the Atlantic.

The sixties witnessed the emergence of new trends in children's playthings, with their own distinctive lapses in taste.[8] The normally self-confident Disney and Hasbro corporations stumbled badly when they rolled out the rubbery material known as Flubber in the early sixties. Flubber was 'a puttylike compound based on the magic material in *Son of Flubber*, sequel to *The Absent Minded Professor* . . . From Disney to Hasbro to you – the new kid craze,' the catalogue copy proclaimed. 'Flubber is a new parent-approved material that is non-toxic and will not stain . . . Flubber acts amazing. It bounces so high. It floats like a boat. It flows and moves.' Hasbro's compound was backed by television commercials, Sunday comics and a comic book, heady stuff in an era before multimillion-dollar campaigns were common. However, the US Food and Drug Administration began investigating reports that the compounds, a mix of synthetic rubber and mineral oil, gave some children sore throats and caused others to break out in full-body rashes. In March 1963 a Kansas housewife filed a $104,000 lawsuit, an enormous sum at the time, claiming Flubber had caused rashes so severe on her and her three-year-old son that both required hospital treatment. Hasbro recalled its compound and stopped all production. Allegedly unable to dispose of it at sea (Flubber floated) or burn it, Hasbro buried several tons of the stuff behind a warehouse and paved it over for a parking lot. Company legend three decades later still held that on the hottest summer days Flubber oozed through cracks in the pavement.[9]

Extravagant as this failure had been, it was small beer compared with the cartoon show *Hot Wheels*. This programme, sponsored by the Mattel company, was the first of many full-length advertisements for toys, a new trend that left a permanent mark on entertainment for children. No longer did programming instigate product; now product was the motivation for programming. In 1969 a competitor of Mattel brought a claim against the ABC Network charging that *Hot Wheels* was nothing more than a thirty-minute commercial for Mattel's toys. The Federal Communications Commission ruled that some parts of the programme could indeed be considered as commercial time and expressed concern with this 'disturbing pattern'.[10] ABC dropped the programme, but many more such cartoons were to follow in the decades ahead.

The nexus between children's television and profits had been exposed with stark clarity by this case, triggering a round of soul-searching among policy-makers, who feared losing a generation of youngsters to high-pressure sales tactics. It also stimulated the formation of child protection movements in the USA, such as Action for Children's Television. At around the same time in the UK Mary Whitehouse was taking up the cudgels in a rather different way, with mixed results. But despite the differences in ideology, there was common agreement that children were not to be treated as consumers-in-miniature but as a vulnerable group requiring special attention and protection.

Despite these efforts, the marketing industry pressed relentlessly forward, and it continues to do so. Globalization and the explosive expansion of the internet have opened new frontiers for toy manufacturers. They are no longer at the mercy of seasonal trends, characterized by sharp peaks at Christmastime. Nowadays toys are sold year-round. In London the epicentre of toy retailing is on Regent Street, where the venerable Hamleys stands alongside the more recent Disney and Warner Bros toy stores, both monuments to corporate success and brash self-confidence and also a perfect demonstration of the power of 'synergy' – they complement rather than compete with one another, as young children insist on making a special stop at each establishment in turn, dragging their parents along.

In theory, this marketing revolution should have been a bonanza for manufacturers. Strange as it may seem, however, the nineties were no picnic for toy companies. There are still constraints on youngsters' spending power, as children under eighteen are not generally eligible to use credit cards. Like many other 'dotcom' enterprises, internet toy companies (such as eToys) often foundered, unable to turn a profit. Even bricks-and-mortar toy manufacturers saw their bottom line eroded by the mysterious phenomenon of 'age compression', in which long-accepted age ranges for toys and games have shrunk in a downward direction. Girls who played with Barbie dolls into their early teens now toss them aside much earlier, lured by make-up, earrings and other questionable tokens of adolescence. Video games and computers (and the world wide web itself) compete with toys for kids' attention. Fickle tastes go hand-in-hand with dwindling attention spans. As one commentator put it, 'The vagaries of playground peer pressure . . . can destroy fads in the space of a morning recess.'[11] In the USA corporate marketing strategies are further complicated by the fact that American teenagers typically hold down a job (for up to forty hours a week, to pay for petrol and insurance on their cars) and are thus harder for advertisers to reach and pin down.

Thus, the overall economic picture for the merchandising industry is decidedly mixed, and picking the winners and losers in the toy business is no easy task. Toy manufacturers have not had everything their own way; however, their marketing techniques and strategies have evolved beyond recognition. Early merchandising methods were unsystematic, comparatively unsophisticated and after-the-fact. Today the marketing campaign is locked firmly in place well before a television programme or movie is released; the tail is wagging the dog. Entertainment executives and toy manufacturers plan their campaigns down to the last detail, well in advance, leaving nothing to chance.

Even the ultra-cautious BBC has not been unaffected by these tectonic shifts. Though some might mourn the loss of the Beeb's earlier gentility, there can be no question that the organization has been dragged into the twenty-first century, financially speaking. The BBC's own odyssey through the world of marketing beautifully epitomizes the free market's impact on staid, traditionalist institutions and their attitudes.

The old BBC seldom exploited its corporate assets to the hilt. Lord Reith's Corporation saw itself primarily as an arbiter and improver of public taste; consumer choice and autonomy were hardly priorities. But as early as 1952 Harry Corbett's puppet Sooty was a 'must-have' toy.[12] And the Beeb itself, diffidently and indirectly, gradually became involved in marketing.

> At first, many complex problems hindered [sales of radio and television programmes], including union and copyright restrictions. By the sixties, the technical situation had improved and in 1958 a Business Manager (Television Programmes) had been appointed. His job was to 'stimulate production of television programmes on film in Britain and the Commonwealth countries' . . . All this work began to develop more vigorously from 1960 onwards, the year when BBC Television Promotions was established with a General Manager. In the following year, the more appropriate name of BBC Enterprises was adopted. In its first year the new department sold 550 programmes overseas and followed this in 1961 with 1,200 sales to more than 50 countries. Many foreign viewers were now able to enjoy series such series as *Face to Face* and *Hancock's Half-Hour* . . . The BBC's major step into an increasingly market-oriented culture came in 1979, the year of Mrs Thatcher's victory, when BBC Enterprises became BBC Enterprises Ltd, a subsidiary company wholly owned by the BBC. By 1982, turnover had increased from £234,000 in 1960 to £23 million, and there were now nine sales divisions, including film, records and tapes, merchandising, home video, education and training, and exhibitions.[13]

Across the Atlantic, the television marketing industry was in ferment. In the early years of television 'marketing' had meant selling television sets and building up a reliable pool of viewers. However, 'within a narrow period of four years, between 1948 and 1952, television ownership in America rose from a few thousand to 15 million'.[14] As time passed, US television executives began to grasp the importance of Saturday morning cartoon programming as a window into the hearts and minds of child viewers. Artistic standards evaporated as the race was on to deliver up young consumers to the advertising industry.

> The networks discovered ways of keeping down the costs of children's programming: Cartoons made expressly for television using cost-saving, 'limited animation' techniques became a Saturday morning staple, and further savings were realized by repeating each new episode many times . . . The formula proved successful, and toy, cereal, and candy makers quickly found that Saturday morning advertising was an effective way to sell their products to a national audience of children . . . Saturday morning had become virtually a carbon copy of prime-time except that the target audience for both programs and commercials was not adults but children between the ages of two and twelve.[15]

According to industry literature today, children are primarily seen as constituting three types of consumer: primary markets, future markets and influence markets.[16] Future markets are to be developed throughout adolescence by the cultivation of brand loyalty. The influence market is activated through 'pester-power' (a fancy term for driving parents up the wall).

The only possible conclusion, then, is that the 'ennobling' mission ascribed to children's television in the post-war period is a relic of the past. Today, television networks, advertisers and licence-holders make systematic efforts to solicit the wishes and views of children; in this sense ideas flow in both directions, each side responding to cues from the other. Focus groups for youngsters are common.

For those in the toy business who successfully ride the roller-coaster, success brings huge rewards. The *Sunday Times* recently profiled one leading merchandiser: 'The "saggy old cloth cat" called Bagpuss sitting in a toy shop near you is the latest offering from Golden Bear Products, the Telford-based soft toy manufacturer with a Midas touch. John Hales, the company's founder, set up on his own in 1979 after working for the Chad Valley toy company, and unsuccessful spells as a policeman (he made no arrests) . . . John Hales and his family have an 80% stake, worth £96 million.'[17]

Not every entrepreneur has had a smooth ride. Back in the early eighties in California, Leib Ostrow launched a record label for kids, aimed at reissuing high-quality music for children. Music for Little People was formally launched in 1985. At first all went well, but the company suffered from mysterious cash shortages; soon the Internal Revenue Service came calling, and the awful truth of the company's bungled finances came to light. Mr Ostrow fired his bookkeeper, but not before the fellow in question had helpfully chucked the company books down a ravine. Mr Ostrow's creditors were sympathetic, recognizing his innocence and his value to the company, and today the founder of Music for Little People is back in business, older but wiser.[18]

On both sides of the Atlantic, thanks to the widespread acceptance of marketing as a fact of life, combined with the worldwide corporate reach provided by satellite television, cable and video, shows such as *Teletubbies* and *Bob the Builder* were fully exploiting their commercial power by the nineties.[19] A new and complex web of financial relationships has developed between the television studios, advertisers and brand licensees. 'The high-risk nature of production . . . has encouraged sharing the investment costs [among] as many agents as possible: Manufacturer, advertiser, licensing agent, syndication company, distribution house, and television stations all become a part of the investment process. This ensures profitability, spreads economic risk, and opens new markets.'[20]

This manifestation of globalization has not gone unchallenged. There have been angry protests around the world from parents and politicians, objecting to the spread of commercialization on moral and ethical grounds. Anxious to forestall such complaints, the key players in the industry make attempts to blunt the capitalist edges of their activities. They seek to imbue their sales pitches with profound ethical sentiments. The goods or services they sell to kids are always (they insist) wholesome – never simply predicated on sex and violence. A prime example is pop star Britney Spears, high priestess of the new generation of singing Lolitas. She attracted considerable attention by exposing her midriff in skimpy outfits on television screens all over the world, but her mother stoutly defended her innocence and integrity, insisting that her clothes are 'just a costume'.[21]

Disney is ever vigilant in the protection of its image. On 11 May 2001 Associated Press announced Disney's unveiling of its first violent computer game, 'Atlantis: Trial by Fire'. 'We don't want to glorify the weapon,' said Jamie Berger, director of marketing at Disney Interactive. 'We wanted it to have more than just pure combat, wanted a broader set of skills required. The tools are literally tools, things that are useful in a problem-solving context and not just tools for conflict.'

For slightly different reasons, the BBC is also careful to offer a moral justification for its commercial enterprises. On 3 January 2001 the BBC's website reported that 'Profits from the BBC Worldwide Division are ploughed back into programming. Last year £82 million were put back into the BBC's coffers. BBC Worldwide chief executive Rupert Gavin said: "It's wonderful to see how popular BBC products are and, because we reinvest the profits in BBC programmes, it's a wonderful boost for the licence payer as well."'

Marketers may reasonably take issue with the automatic assumption that they are engaging in unethical practices or exploiting inno-cent children. Merchandising is not necessarily detrimental to children. Commercials are an intrinsic part of our culture, and the children of today are the shoppers of tomorrow; so perhaps it can be argued that the sooner they learn to become discriminating con-sumers the better. Besides, advertisements can give great pleasure. Some classic commercials are so good that, once seen, they are never forgotten.

This is especially important in establishing brand identity and brand loyalty. And young people 'love brands. Brands delight. Brands provide a badge of identity. Brands are enablers. Brands are passports to global culture. Brands are tickets to success. Brands embody all the good values that life has to offer: fun, attractiveness, and opportunity for a better life.'[22] To this day my son Neil remembers the landmark slo-gans of yesteryear, including 'Graded grains make finer flour' (which advertised Homepride).[23] Neil's generation chortled at the long-run-ning 'Secret Lemonade Drinker' campaigns of the seventies and eighties (R Whites Lemonade).[24] The Martians in the Smash instant potato commercials (1973), who made fun of Planet Earth's cumber-some practice of mashing spuds by hand, illustrate another point – that traditional distinctions between categories of marketing no longer hold, for we live in a multimedia world. These were advertise-ments for food, but they employed the services of an actor who had provided the voice for one of the Daleks in *Dr Who*.[25]

If brands please children, they also delight large corporations. And with skilful advertising it is possible to restore treasured brands that have become flabby, quaint and obsolete. The late Canadian writer Eric Burdick (author of *I'm Coming, Virginia, Old Rag Bone* and *How to Become a Complete Alcoholic*), who had started out in adver-tising, argued that all brands must have a 'unique selling point' or USP, though with some products it is by no means clear what that USP is. In the sixties I gave my children Ribena and Lucozade to drink when they were sick (we were less conscious of the impact of sugary drinks on teeth in those days). This connection with sickness (rammed home with the slogan 'Lucozade Aids Recovery') subsequently became an embarrassment, so the makers of Lucozade worked hard to shake off this USP. Drawing upon the wealth of resources available to advertisers in the multimedia world, they took the decision to 'hire' cyber-adventuress Lara Croft to re-pitch the fizzy drink. (We shall have more to say about Lara Croft's magical powers of resurrection.)

The belief that advertising campaigns invariably erode family values and domestic harmony, driving a wedge between children and their parents, is open to question. A 24 October 1962 *Daily Express* advertisement for Kraft Dairylea announced a competition in which the first prize was 'a £2,000 holiday in Los Angeles, America, for Mother, Father, and the children; visiting Disneyland (the world's most famous children's playground). Maybe you will take your children by Pan American jet to fabulous America!' The advertising pitch is directed at parents, and Father is explicitly invited to join in. Family values are not only evoked but reinforced.

After discussing the subject with innumerable solid citizens who grew up surrounded by merchandising campaigns, I cannot escape the conclusion that they were altogether unscathed by their exposure to them. Elizabeth Ray, writer and widow of wine expert Cyril Ray, told me that she has fond memories of collecting Huntley and Palmer miniature biscuit tins in the thirties. My late husband Brian Inglis, not a man generally known for bursting into song, was none the less given to singing the theme from the Ovaltinies' Club:

> At games and sports we're more than keen,
> No merrier children should be seen,
> Because we all drink Ovaltine,
> We're happy girls and boys![26]

And Annabel Davis, press officer for Plan International (the 'Adopt-a-Child' charity with headquarters in north-west London), remembered that her favourite toy as a three- and four-year-old had been Humpty Dumpty; she points out that *Play School* was reassuringly protective of Humpty: 'He was never allowed to fall off the wall.' These people all thought of toys and collectable commercial objects as valuable commodities in their youth, marks of acceptance, badges of membership.

Commercial exploitation of artistic material has been contentious in the rock music industry, where many celebrities have ostentatiously rejected offers to participate in product placement and promotional ventures. A notable example is Canadian rocker Neil Young, who fulminated against commercial tie-ins in the title track to *This Note's for You*.[27] In his plaintive voice, he proclaims his refusal to endorse Pepsi, Coca-Cola, Budweiser or Miller.

Commercials aimed at children are an especially sensitive subject, particularly with politicians and parents. Yet parents are every bit as malleable and impressionable as their children. They are hardly Lone Rangers protecting their offspring from advertising; if anything, they are deeply implicated in the entire exercise. Wilson Brian Key, in his magisterial account of sixties' advertising techniques, *Subliminal Seduction*, tells us why: 'Television is a major consideration as to *when the family goes to bed* (after the 11 p.m. news), *when the family goes to the toilet or engages in conversation* (during commercials), *when the family eats or snacks, what family activities will be on weekends* (relative to games, program schedules, and sport seasons), *when parents do or do not have sex . . .*'[28]

Nor are parental aspirations, as reflected in television advertising targeted at grown-ups, always noble and ethical.

This is difficult to believe – especially after absorbing an evening of what appears to be total absurdity as men and women discuss their constipation, bad breath, body odour, smelly feet, insomnia, backaches, indigestion, and an incredible assortment of psychosomatic ailments before millions of viewers. The women on television commercials appear as neurotic morons whose main life interest involves their never-quite-white laundry, their never-quite-comfortable girdles and brassieres, their relentless search for a kitchen free of stains, germs, odours, and unsightly linoleum scratches and – the greatest banality of them all – the struggle to obtain really soft toilet tissue.[29]

In any event, parents may not need any special nagging from kids to open their purse-strings. Mums and dads buy expensive gifts for their children for a variety of reasons: treats to salve parental guilt at working long hours and neglecting their offspring; videos to babysit the kids while they catch up on sleep; and bribes to buy the children's silence. This is not a new phenomenon. In 1948 Jack Gould, the first television critic of the *New York Times*, described the impact of the new medium: 'Children's hours of television admittedly are an insidious narcotic to the parent. With the tots fanned out on the floor in front of the receiver, a strange if wonderful quiet seems at hand.'[30]

Another potent stimulus to large-scale toy purchasing is the desire the keep up with the Joneses. The 9 June 1994 edition of the *Washington Post* carried a story about the toy-buying season at major toy stores in the USA: frantic parents prowled the aisles in search of the latest Power Rangers gadgetry for their offspring. At one point, parents menacingly encircled a hapless truck driver who had just pulled up in the loading bay, demanding information about his payload and whether it contained the fashionable toy *du jour*. Other parents vaulted security fences to jump the queue waiting outside the shops before opening time. Rereading these and other newspaper accounts, a common theme emerges: these parental scavenger hunts are a form of guerrilla warfare.[31]

I have tried so far to accentuate the positive in my account of advertising aimed at children. Of course the picture is mixed, and the merchandising industry has come in for much well-deserved criticism. So what are the undesirable features of this business? Wilson Brian Key emphasizes its cold calculation:

> Television commercials are the most carefully produced material in the entire field of mass communication. In a 60-second commercial, every single second . . . of both audio and visual content has been precision engineered to accomplish a specific end – sell the product. And television commercials work . . . and the theory suggests that they are most effective with people who believe themselves to be the most indifferent to their appeals . . . An effective TV commercial is purposefully designed to insult the viewer's conscious intelligence, thereby penetrating his defenses.[32]

It is often argued that children are connoisseurs of advertising – savvy viewers capable of separating the wheat from the chaff. But this reassuring view may in fact be dangerously misleading and complacent. Key's arguments resonate powerfully with parents' instincts concerning the pernicious (but often invisible) influences surrounding their children. And time and again legions of concerned parents (usually mothers) have taken up arms against them. Parental backlashes are a recurrent feature in the history of child merchandising.

A recent movement, the Motherhood Project, was launched on Mother's Day 2001 under the auspices of the Institute for American Values. The campaign urges advertisers to exercise restraint; it accuses them of employing insidious technologies and powerful tools that infiltrate children's minds and undermine fundamental parental roles. The campaign's manifesto[33] explicitly attacks the 'if-it-feels-good-do-it' philosophy of advertising. The mothers say that they will turn their homes into commerce-free zones and that they will resist 'branding'.

They warn that they will not allow their kids to be subjects of market research. The material is written in strikingly traditionalist language; the angry mothers contrast the business world with the world at home (the 'Money World' versus the 'Motherworld'). Their 'separate spheres' language would not be out of place in a Victorian tract on the virtues of motherhood. Lest we underestimate these formidable ladies, note that they have a clear-cut set of demands:

Mothers' Code for Advertisers

- No advertising, marketing, or market research in schools, including high schools.
- No targeting of advertising and marketing at children under the age of eight.
- No product placement in movies and media programs targeted at children and adolescents.
- No behavioral science research to develop advertising and marketing aimed at children and adolescents.
- No advertising and marketing directed at children and adolescents that promotes an ethic of selfishness and a focus on instant gratification.
- Good faith efforts to reduce sponsorship of gratuitously sexual and/or violent programming likely to be watched by children.

The arguments advanced earlier in defence of advertising cut no ice with these mothers, whose convictions have the status of revealed truth.[34] What makes these women tick? What is the root cause of their anxiety about businesses' efforts to convert their children into the consumers of the future?

The stakes are certainly high. Television is an enormously important and powerful influence on the young child: it gives pleasure that is subtly bound up with some of the child's most primitive gratifications.[35] Advertising hooks its claws into children at the most fundamental level. It connects with their most basic bodily functions: eating, drinking, listening to music, personal hygiene, a desire to be popular, their urge to be loved, their emerging sexuality. Thus advertising challenges parental authority both directly and indirectly.

To deal with the most obvious criticisms first – those pertaining to deceptive advertising and the promotion of aggressive behaviour – it is undeniable that many of the claims made in adverts for children are outright lies. The crusader for better nutrition, Robert B. Choate, told the US Senate's consumer committee in July 1970 that breakfast cereal makers dupe young children about the real nutritional value of cereals:

> Their koala bear, says Cocoa Krispies, gives you good wind; and their Sugar Smacks suggests that it can remove the hole from your paddle and get you correctly to anticipate the next bounce of the ball. Kellogg's Apple Jacks so invigorates that kids roll up hill, and General Mills' Cheerios 'makes you feel groovy all morning long.' General Foods' Honeycombs bribes you with an offer of fast automobiles, and Lucky Charms is described as 'the frosted oat cereal with hearts, moons, stars, clovers . . . they're magically delicious.'[36]

The Lion and Lamb project campaigns against the peddling of violence to kids, publishing a list entitled 'Dirty Dozen – 12 Toys to Avoid' on its website. One of the worst offenders is the 'Goldberg Smash and Bash Game' (Tiger/Hasbro).

> Recommended age: 5 +. Description: An electronic talking action figure based on a World Championship Wrestling figure. Why we chose it: The packaging suggests that preschoolers act out wrestling moves with this toy. 'You must quickly react by smashing his head, bashing his chest or twisting his arm before he comes at you with his next move,' the package says. Children learn by imitation.[37]

Today advertising is criticized for its bluntness. In earlier generations it was criticized for its deviousness. During the Vietnam era the major concern was with subliminal advertising and mind control; it was believed that advertisers held the key to tapping into consumers' unconscious minds. This idea generated many preposterous theories. Wilson Brian Key mentions the invariable use at that time of ice cubes in print advertisements for alcoholic beverages (ice cubes are difficult to shoot, incidentally, because they melt away under the heat of studio arc lights). Some commentators believed the cubes were deliberately shaped and photographed to hint at the female anatomy, especially breasts. Similarly, in the American South fundamentalist watchdog organizations were up in arms about rock music and its baneful influence on kids, suspecting that Satanic messages were imprinted on LP records; these messages could supposedly be detected only if the music were played backwards, a technique known as backward masking or 'backmasking'.

The issue of subliminal effects resurfaced recently during the Pokémon craze in Japan. The culprit was said to be the *Pokémon* television show, which used a flashing strobe-like technique in its animation: 'In December 1997, up to 12,000 Japanese children reported illnesses ranging from nausea to seizures . . . children went into a trance-like state, similar to hypnosis, complaining of shortness of breath, nausea, and bad vision . . . News of the attacks shot through Japan . . . several stations replayed the flashing sequence, whereupon even more children fell ill and sought medical attention.'[38] Parents are justified in feeling shocked and betrayed in such cases.

As befits our multimedia world, Pokémon characters come in many forms, most notably trading cards. To their supporters, Pokémon cards teach kids the importance of free markets and price-setting. There's a down side to all this Thatcherite happy-talk, of course. Pokémon 'thousand-aires' also learn about stock exchange crashes in miniature; you can make money only if you sell your holdings at the right time.[39] There have been shortages of certain Pokémon collectables, sending children (and their harried parents) off on wild goose chases in a fruitless effort to track down the missing item. More sinisterly, could it be that the manufacturer produces too few of certain Pokémon creatures, thereby concocting what economists call a 'contrived scarcity'? Do parents really want their little ones used as guinea-pigs in a real-life experiment in monetarist economics? Are they not sacrificing their innocence too soon? Whatever happened to allowing a child's innocent imagination to roam free?

Few would argue that many toys today fail to encourage imaginative play. In the past a boy or girl could invest a Teddy (or even a Sooty) with a rich and complex inner life of its own; today, Disney and Warner Bros toy characters come with a built-in history and characteristics. This encourages passivity, triggering short attention spans and boredom. Since toys and video games compete for children's time with more traditional pursuits such as reading (which requires sustained concentration and self-discipline), are the latest generation of kids prone to 'aliteracy' – the state of being functionally able to read but never picking up a book and reading it from cover to cover?

One of the most ferocious challenges to the worldwide cavalcade of kiddie advertising has to do with the treatment of girls on television and in other spheres of the entertainment industry. Here the historical record has its ups and downs. Following the doleful helplessness of Little Weed and Looby Loo in *Watch With Mother*, by the sixties and seventies we began to spot the occasional role models for girls (for instance, the characters of Zoe and Jo in *Dr Who*). And despite all the chatter about 'girl power' in the nineties, true girl power originated three decades earlier with the advent of such singers as Dusty Springfield, who were gifted performers and staunchly independent artists in their own right.

Today, the concept of 'girl power' is perhaps best embodied by Sarah Michelle Gellar, star of *Buffy the Vampire Slayer*, the internationally acclaimed television show. Buffy may be attractive, but she is not primarily a sex symbol; she is self-sufficient, adept at self-defence, and in the show's plot the safety of the world is in some sense in her hands. Another female icon, who has undergone a series of transmutations in the interests of commercial exploitation, is Lara Croft. She began as a print cartoon character, and was then taken up in a kidvid game; she subsequently became a pitchwoman for a soft drink; and most recently was brought to the big screen (*Tomb Raider*, 2001), played this time by a real actress (Angelina Jolie, who incidentally makes a powerful argument in favour of the superiority of flesh-and-blood women).

The blend of good intentions and filthy lucre, long a hallmark of children's television all over the world, is exemplified by the extravagant success of the nineties' mega-hit *Barney and Friends*. This cuddly Mesozoic monster has had a chequered history. Turning the normal marketing process upside-down, Barney started life as a video.[40] The show, first broadcast in 1992, did wonders for PBS's children's programming ratings, but in the early days the cold cash went not to PBS but to the show's licensee, the Lyons Group. Another licensee noted: 'Adults think PBS is sharing in the pot . . . They get zip, zilch, nada.'[41] 'According to some reports, the Corporation for Public Broadcasting and PBS funded between 40% and 50% of *Barney* production costs (approximately $4 million of $14.5 million total production costs) over its first three seasons . . . yet only received fees from *Barney* tapes and compact disks . . . missing out on "Barneymania" and a percentage of the estimated $500 million per year in retail sales.'[42]

Normally, of course, the marketing process begins with a television programme's first show. A cherished children's programme may be converted to video or in some instances into a motion picture, and the transfer to the big-screen format can then lead to a profitable series of spin-off movies (often confusingly called a franchise). The *Superman* and *Batman* movies are examples. But movie spin-offs are not always a success. The motion picture of *Lost in Space* (1998, starring William

169

Hurt, Gary Oldman and Heather Graham) did retain some of the original actors in cameo roles, to appease connoisseurs of the original series, but otherwise the movie version had very little in common with the television show. It was a giant video game for the big screen; the delicate whimsy of the television programme was crushed and ruined. My son, a diehard fan of the original (and an admirer of Jonathan Harris in the role of Zachary Smith), reported watching the movie with his head buried in his hands. The bitterness of the betrayed television nostalgia buff knows no bounds.[43]

The globalization of children's entertainment was at first restrained by the quotas individual countries imposed on imported television programmes, but this system was effectively circumvented by the spread of satellite, cable television and video. And language was not to be a barrier to the penetration of foreign markets, because production companies took to making foreign-language versions of their shows, sometimes with rewritten scripts and in some cases with entirely new characters. Here again Oliver Postgate was a pioneer, as he describes in his autobiography:

> I took an episode of *The Clangers* to the 1984 conference in Germany and showed it to the participants without my voice-over. Afterwards I asked them whether they had been able to understand what the Clangers were saying.
> 'But of course,' said some. 'They are speaking perfect German.'
> 'But no,' said another. 'That is not so. They spoke only Swedish.'[44]

The Children's Television Workshop (CTW), which produces *Sesame Street*, is another expert in the art of making a global product. However, it came to grief when it attempted to adapt its product for the Middle East, believing it could appeal both to Israeli and Palestinian children simultaneously and thus become a force for peace and reconciliation. Providing the narration in a blend of Arabic and

Hebrew was risky enough, because each side tends to regard the other's language as the 'language of death'. But its attempt to introduce a new character in the form of a thoughtful Israeli soldier, designed to humanize the Israelis in the eyes of Palestinian viewers, was hastily scrapped when CTW's own rulebook was found to forbid military plotlines of any kind.[45]

By the early eighties over 5 per cent of households had a video recorder, but by the nineties this figure had risen to 64 per cent globally. 'Self-scheduling' by the viewer gained in popularity. A huge new market opened up for the television networks based on Baby Boomer nostalgia. Middle-aged men and women are willing to pay good money to relive their childhood memories. Dust-strewn movie vaults hold tremendous commercial value, yet the major networks were slow to awaken to the scale of the treasure trove on their hands.

What happens if those treasures have been mutilated or destroyed? The BBC, which did not see the video revolution coming and threw out much of its back-list, has recently been playing a frantic game of catch-up. A determined effort is under way to dig up surviving copies of classic television episodes, long thought destroyed:

> BBC bosses are hoping that fans who recorded the shows when they were first broadcast will hand them over to complete the archives. They also plan to jog the memories of former members of staff who may have absent-mindedly stockpiled copies at home ... Until recently, 13 out of 20 episodes of the 1960s' series *The Likely Lads* were missing, but a team of amateur collectors called Kaleidoscope uncovered an edition called 'The Last of the Big Spenders'. The show was first broadcast on July 7, 1965, and features a youthful Wendy Richard as a guest actress, alongside the stars of the series, James Bolam and Rodney Bewes.[46]

A spare copy of one of the finest early *Dr Who* serials, 'The Tomb of the Daleks', produced in the late sixties, was discovered quite by accident. And even a sci-fi serial with individual episodes missing can be patched up and sold. In a video version of 'The Invasion', another Patrick Troughton serial (from 1968), Nicholas Courtney (Lethbridge-Stewart in the original) provided brief summaries of the long-lost episodes to fill in the gaps. In 'The Ice Monsters' still camera footage from the missing episodes was combined with surviving audio soundtracks to provide a modicum of continuity.

The record of US television companies is hardly better. Johnny Carson's first appearance on *The Tonight Show* and the first two Superbowls (American football finals) are lost for good.[47] And a recent article on *The Flintstones* in *USA Today* pointed out that the CBS network had little sense of history or future commercial potential when it was making and first showing the series.[48]

The preservation and study of ancient footage are about more than just commercial value. For instance, researchers digging through the archives learned that Joe Barbera discreetly changed Fred Flintstone's original war cry of 'Yahoo!' to 'Yabba-dabba doo!' after one of the voiceover people made the suggestion.[49]

Prudent management of television and movie archives is not simply a question of wringing out every last penny of profit. It is also about protecting the brand and shielding it from exposure that might sabotage its present and future commercial potential. The Cartoon Network learnt this to its chagrin when it acquired the rights to all the Bugs Bunny cartoons. In early May 2001 it announced that it would celebrate by holding a marathon 49-hour broadcast of the entire Bugs canon – the first complete airing ever. Then it took a closer look at its latest acquisition. The 'wascally wabbit' had been distinctly lacking in political correctness, especially during the Second World War:

All This and Rabbit Stew is one of 12 cartoons pulled from the Bugs festival. . . . It is a seven-minute short, produced in 1941, in which a black hunter stalks Bugs Bunny. The hunter, all massive lips and shuffling feet, is the sort of crude stereotype guaranteed to generate outrage today. The 11 other banned cartoons, created between 1941 and 1960, contain similarly provocative images: bloodthirsty Native Americans, bumbling Japanese soldiers, savage Eskimos. Bugs's many encounters with French, Italian, and Irish stereotypes will run uncensored . . . But cartoons, like other unruly eruptions from the subconscious, are likely to frustrate the efforts of studios, networks, and other grown-up institutions to control them.[50]

Sensitivity to racism is one thing, but self-appointed arbiters of public morality find fault with classic cartoons on other grounds. Kimberly Thompson and Fumie Yokota of the Harvard School of Public Health found that of a sample of eighty-one classic animated features nearly half showed a casual approach towards alcohol or smoking.[51] For example, *The Little Mermaid* showed seven seconds of smoking. These authors were not recommending censorship of the classic cartoons (at least not explicitly), but they did suggest that parents discuss the dangers with their youngsters. In its Weekend section, the *Washington Post* routinely warns parents against tobacco use in movies that children may see.

That there is substantial untapped demand for video reissues of long-ago television shows is not in dispute. However, identifying the precise nature of that consumer interest is a more complex task. Is watching an old show an act of aesthetic appreciation, or is it more a question of wallowing in nostalgia? What happens when a consumer picks up a video of a cherished childhood programme and is disillusioned with the results?

Early attempts to recycle the BBC's kiddie vault met with mixed critical results. Writing in the 7–13 January 1989 edition of the *Radio Times*, Libby Purves and her own focus group of toddlers were underwhelmed by the new *Watch With Mother* releases. Even *Rag, Tag and Bobtail* (arguably the liveliest of the stable) failed to kindle much excitement:

> It must be said that *Andy Pandy* was, and is, the dullest show on earth . . . There is no point being nostalgic. It was all good pioneering stuff in its day: it made possible the birth of Postman Pat, Bertha, and Charlie Chalk. But although children are eternally fresh, television itself has lost its youth. It will never again serve quite the kind of homely pie that *Watch With Mother* used to make. Thank goodness!

Children and grown-ups bring entirely different sets of expectations and criteria to the television viewing process. The ancient and noble art of puppetry fails to impress modern-day youngsters, who expect electronic gadgetry and whizz-bang special effects. When confronted with pioneer kiddie shows, younger viewers are likely to chafe at the old technology, the slow pace and especially the absence of colour. Older and younger viewers may evaluate the black-and-white versus colour issue differently, as Victor Lewis-Smith explained: 'Just as the colour footage of Adolf [Hitler] and his chums lacked the menace of those grim monochrome Nazi images . . . so my first glimpse of red, blue and gold Daleks (with amber blinkers) suddenly robbed them of the power they'd once had over me. On the family black-and-white television, they'd seemed to embody all that was evil . . .'[52]

Some old shows, and some characters, hold up better than others, forging intense bonds of loyalty that withstand the passage of time. A recent 'where-are-they-now' episode of the US programme *Entertainment Tonight* broadcast old footage of a gaunt and emaciated Bill Bixby in 1993, dying of terminal cancer. Bixby was known and loved by generations of young people, beginning with *The Courtship of Eddie's Father* in the sixties and ending with *The Incredible Hulk*, where he came into his own in the role of Dr David Banner. To watch Bixby break down in tears on camera, sobbing at the cruel fate that lay in store for him, was to grieve over the loss of an old and trusted friend.

And some old programmes are so glorious that they transcend any amount of bungling ineptitude by studio executives. The slow emergence of the Cybermen from their icy catacomb in the 1967 *Dr Who* episode 'The Tomb of the Cybermen' is a moment of bloodcurdling horror that no interval of time can neutralize. The best of children's television has this power. And that is why it is about more than merchandising.

7

The Emotional Effects of Television on Children

Parental Guidance

'Television's effect on children has been a source of controversy ever since the first kid sat down and watched glassy-eyed as Mighty Mouse roared down from outer space.' – Mary W. Quigley[1]

Television has held children in its thrall since it was first broadcast over fifty years ago. Television producers have always been deeply satisfied with its popularity with the young and only mildly concerned about its possibly deleterious effects. They coasted along for decades largely ignoring what the psychiatrists and watchdogs had been saying about its harmful aspects.

However, in 1993 they were forced to wake up, in the USA at any rate, because their revenue stream was threatened. In the summer of that year parents in America began hearing about the V-chip, a computer chip that would be installed in television sets to intercept the electronic coding of offensive programmes and block them. A *New York Times* journalist, Edmund L. Andrews, welcomed it enthusiastically: 'It's cheap. It's easy. It's controversial: the broadcasters hate it.'[2] They especially hated the prospect that government sanctions (such as the refusal of corporate licence renewals) might follow if they did not comply.

On 14 October 1993 US Attorney General Janet Reno endorsed anti-violence legislation which mandated the inclusion of V-chip technology in all new television sets, provoking a storm of protest from the advertising and entertainment industry. There were loud claims that the First Amendment (enshrining the right to free speech) was being undermined. A feature in *Advertising Age*, published the day after the new law's passing, greeted it ferociously with the headline 'No! to feds monitoring television'; the article went on to say that 68 per cent of advertising professionals responding to the magazine's poll condemned legislative attempts to curb television violence.[3] As Mandy Rice-Davies remarked during the Profumo crisis in Britain, 'They would, wouldn't they?'

The US legislation had its admirers in the British government, including Virginia Bottomley, UK Minister for Health in John Major's 1991 Cabinet. But most British media professionals agreed that the V-chip was too strong a dose of medicine, unnecessary and perhaps even undemocratic; and the law was not enacted here. As Eric Wilsher of *European Satellite Users* magazine told me: 'We let parents do the protecting here. We're comfortable with the nine o'clock watershed, and parents can PIN control any adult material on Sky Television. If the PIN isn't used, you just get a blank screen, so parents keep the PIN number to themselves. As for terrestrial television – which is the extra set in the bedroom that children usually watch – most parents feel easy with the watershed protection.'

In France there is a system of controlled viewing: colour codes advise parents about unsuitable 'adult' programmes (a red dot warns of nakedness in an adult show, for instance). In Canada the broadcasters themselves have agreed to a code of self-regulation. Foreign critics of US television often concede that V-chip censorship may be necessary there, since some of the worst children's television fare emanates from the USA; they cite the *Ninja Turtles* and *Mighty Morphin Power Rangers*, which are the two worst examples of the glorification of violence. This is of course a harsh verdict on the nation which has also given birth to such charming pre-school learning vehicles as *Barney and Friends* and *Sesame Street*.

However, there is cause for concern because children *do* imitate the violence they see on television. A scholar friend of mine said his five-year-old nephew was spending his time high-kicking around the living-room in imitation of the Mighty Morphin Power Rangers, something he had not done before he started watching the programme. Eric Wilsher says his three-year-old jumps off a chair with a great clatter and boom in imitation of any animated space travel he watches. These examples are of course only anecdotal, but the scholarly texts make the same point, particularly with respect to young boys. Elaborate field studies recently conducted by the Indiana University College of Arts and Sciences and the University of Oregon College of Arts and Sciences present plentiful evidence of boys in playgrounds acting 'copy-cat aggressive'. The observations of one pre-school daycare supervisor, Gloria Williams, in a Midwestern suburb, are typical:

> Power Rangers. They play a lot of that. That's their karate. They really try to kick, action, do the flips like the Power Rangers. On the GI Joe they get down and try to hide in little places and spring out on you. Or try to do that Karate Kid move on one foot and all that stuff. Now I do have some girls that will get in there with them. They'll stick with them just like the boys do, you know. Try the karate stuff.[4]

This is not particularly alarming, but other examples are. In October 1993 a woman in Moraine, Ohio, claimed that an episode of *Beavis and Butthead* had inspired her five-year-old son to burn down the family home, killing his two-year-old sister. Its producers, MTV Networks, denied responsibility but promised to modify future episodes to prevent any possible recurrence, for a number of child psychologists had confirmed that the cartoon did adversely influence young children and inspire them to acts of imitative violence.

Although the most assiduous researchers agree that the young imitate the violence they see on television, they stress that it is difficult to assess the scale of the problem. After extensive tests, two distinguished American experts seemed reluctant to be too dogmatic about their findings:

> First, we conclude that television violence seems to be capable of affecting viewers of both sexes and varying ages, social classes, ethnicities, personality characteristics and levels of usual aggressiveness. Second, we conclude that males and females are equally likely to be influenced by exposure but that within each sex those who are more aggressive are more likely to be influenced. We will also advance the tentative conclusion that 'middle-aged' children, those between the ages of about eight and twelve, are somewhat more likely to be affected than are either younger or older youth. Third, we conclude that in actual behavior boys are more likely to be aggressive than are girls, and by definition, delinquents and others who are measured as more aggressive in their daily behavior are more aggressive than are their obvious comparison groups.[5]

In the UK Professor Hilde Himmelweit and her colleagues summed up their findings about children's reactions to television as early as 1958:

> Television can't alter a child's basic personality. It might change some of his opinions and attitudes but definitely not his character. There was no evidence in our study that the kind of personality the child has influences the types of programmes he chooses to watch. A child brings his personality to the set, not the other way round.[6]

Himmelweit and her colleagues also made useful observations about child telly-addicts. They found that, contrary to expectations, the child addict was not an only child or the child whose mother went out to work but the insecure child, the child who was shy and submissive and who made friends with difficulty. The young person who took to television as a refuge had a long inventory of worries, including not getting on well with other children, feeling unpopular, left out of things, different from other children. When asked if they ever asked friends at school to come home and watch television with them, they answered: 'I don't want to bring friends home to watch.'[7]

One of the most elaborate studies conducted in recent times was performed at the University of California School of Medicine in January 1998. Researchers attached electrodes to the arms of young subjects and measured their reactions to a variety of visual images. They found that *implied* violence, such as the appearance of a villain's face, elicited stronger reactions than *actual* violence (a scene showing a stabbing, for instance). Background noises and voices on the soundtrack enhanced fear reactions, too.[8] The history of cinema seems to confirm these findings. Alfred Hitchcock knew the power of combining implied violence with frightening musical scores. No one who has seen the shower curtain and the carving knife and heard the piercing musical accompaniment to the murder scene in *Psycho* can doubt the power of suggestion. The opening musical score of *Dr Who* episodes was also enough to send children scuttling behind the sofa from the sixties on.

No one can reasonably commend imitative violence, but is fear altogether bad? If it were not cathartic and stimulating to the imagination, such plays as Shakespeare's *Hamlet*, *Macbeth* and *Titus Andronicus* would presumably have been banned long ago, along with Grimms' fairy tales and many other children's classics. In fact adults sometimes treasure memories of the fear that books and television provoked in them as children. Nick Magnus, a 35-year-old composer from Hampshire who helped arrange the score for the Beatles musical *All You Need Is Love*, was an ardent fan of composer and television puppet drama producer Roberta Leigh as a child. Leigh made three popular puppet serials in the late fifties and sixties – *Twizzle*, *Torchy* and *Space Patrol* – and collaborated with Gerry Anderson in several episodes of *Torchy*. Nick recalls:

> I used to sprint home from school as fast as I could to see the episodes of *Space Patrol*. It was Roberta Leigh's musical score which had me by the throat. The theme music sent chills through me, and yet I was totally addicted to it. I used to get hooked up to the set so that I could transcribe the musical score on to my own recording machine, and it's a wonder I didn't electrocute myself in those more elementary electrical days. My mother was blissfully unaware of these activities. She was one of those totally trusting, loving mums, in any case. The fear I felt at the *Space Patrol* theme music was a delicious sort of fear. I can't think it did me any serious harm. In fact, it was probably what started me off on my career as a composer. Those sci-fi themes were often fascinating. There were wonderful dissonances and tone colours there.

According to the Indiana and Oregon field workers, two very different educational traditions are especially hostile to the exposure of young children to television: these are the Christian Fundamentalist and the Montessori pre-schools. Both groups feel that television programming, even those PBS children's shows such as *Sesame Street* and *Barney and Friends*, have negative effects on learning. The Christian Fundamentalists feel that *Barney* relies too heavily on magic as a device; for instance, the purple dinosaur's child companions are whisked off to foreign lands (though of course the programme-makers' purpose is to explore the customs and peoples of such places as Mexico, Canada and France, rather than to falsify the realities of travel). The Montessori movement agrees with the Fundamentalists – despite their major differences in other respects – that both *Sesame*

Street and *Barney* blur the line between fantasy and reality too much; for instance, both shows use a combination of Muppets and real people. Montessori teachers do in fact use visual aids such as videos, but these are purely instructive rather than entertaining (such as National Geographic studies of wildlife and ancient civilizations). Ironically, the Christian Fundamentalist schools are slightly more liberal in this respect, since they do tolerate some gentle and non-violent cartoons.

At the other end of the spectrum, the Californian researchers cite carers in a local hospital facility of 138 children, mostly four-year-olds. Two popular teachers, Jean and Gloria, explained their views:

> Jean sees the imitative violence as a natural form of child's play rather than a long-term effect on their minds, and turns it into an opportunity for promoting classroom unity or harmony consensus . . . there is also a willingness to use overt forms of control over the children, to enact punishments or withdraw privileges. TV is useful for both Gloria and Jean as a reward that can be taken away.[9]

Most parents probably think the same way as Jean and Gloria. They also use television to reward or punish their offspring. Many parents try to limit viewing time or at least to offer it as a treat after homework has been completed. Many adhere to the nine o'clock watershed because they want peace and quiet after dinner. They encourage Saturday and Sunday morning viewing so they can have a much-needed lie-in (and weekend morning viewing is largely innocuous, in any case).

While the USA has gone for the V-chip, ignoring those who feel it erodes civil liberties, the rest of the world seems to rely most heavily on parental censure and supervision. Richard Harwood, a *Washington Post* media journalist, argued for the enduring importance of parents' role in an article entitled 'So Many Media, So Little Time' in September 1992:

The ultimate responsibility still rests with parents. The goal should not be – cannot be – to screen out every bad word or karate chop from kids' viewing, but rather to make sure TV doesn't crowd out all the other activities that are part of growing up. These counterbalancing influences – family, friends, school, books – can put TV if not out of the picture at least in the proper focus.[10]

The US government strengthened parents' hands with the Children's Television Act, introduced in 1990 and reinforced in 1996, which decreed that stations must provide three hours of educational programming in order to have their licences renewed by the Federal Communications Commission. (Of course, the mere existence of educational programmes does not guarantee that children will watch them: 54 per cent of American children have a television set in their bedroom, where parents are unlikely to monitor what is being watched.) Support for the government's initiative came from the Center for Media Education, which published a popular pamphlet called *A Parent's Guide to Kids' TV*, outlining some fairly severe rules:

- Limit TV viewing to two hours a day.
- Encourage children to match their reading time with viewing time.
- Ban TV during meals, before school and until homework is done.
- Pre-screen and pre-select shows to make certain they are appropriate.
- Watch with your children and discuss the content of the shows with them afterward.
- Keep a TV diary to know just how much and what everyone is watching.[11]

Admirable as these guidelines are, few parents could easily hold down a full-time job and keep on top of such supervisory duties at the same time. This is especially true of families in which both parents work, now the commonest household arrangement in the West, far outnumbering unemployed single parents living on social security.

In any case, television is often blamed for more of society's ills (rough or impolite children, vandalism, bullying and so on) than is quite fair. Television programmes of the sort produced by PBS, the BBC and Nickelodeon – especially plentiful in the nineties – can actually encourage young schoolchildren to read books, can help them with their literacy skills and even teach them better behaviour (*Barney and Friends*, for instance, regularly exhorts its young viewers to share and to say 'please' and 'thank you').

While there has always been a great deal of breast-beating about the dangers of imitative violence and so forth, there has also been a constant undercurrent of scholarly approval for television's capacity to extend learning boundaries. One US scholar, Pamela M. Almeida, writing in 1977 – by which time afternoon viewing had become a fully integrated feature of home life in America – concluded that 'television as a vehicle for developing positive attitudes toward reading has been under-utilized. By including peer role-modeling of pro-reading behaviors in children's television, a renewed interest and love for reading may be sparked in the children of the electronic generation.'[12]

There has also been a continuing re-evaluation of some of the supposedly negative effects of television programmes, especially a recognition that within limits fear, or mixed emotions (like Nick Magnus's feelings about *Space Patrol*), may be beneficial. In the past child experts often held that strong feelings evoked by the screen would have a desensitizing effect, so that, for example, seeing someone badly hurt in an automobile accident in a television thriller would make children less caring if they witnessed real accidents. Today there is a new conviction that children know the difference between fantasy and reality. As a recent British study puts it:

Emotional responses which are perceived as 'negative' may have 'positive' consequences, for example, in terms of children's learning. Children (and adults) may be extremely distressed by images of disasters or social conflicts shown on the news, but many people would argue that such experiences are a necessary part of becoming an informed citizen. A fear of crime, for example, of the kind that is sometimes seen to be induced by television reporting, may be a necessary prerequisite for crime prevention. Likewise, children's fiction has always prayed on 'negative' responses such as fear and sadness, on the ground that experiencing such emotions in a fictional context can enable children to conquer the fears they experience in real life. In this respect, therefore, we would question the view that consequences of such emotional responses can easily be categorized as either 'positive' or 'negative'.[13]

None the less the 'window in the corner' will probably always be suspected of exerting a baleful influence, whether for its mind-bending qualities or even for its staggering ability to keep children quiet. The latest charge levelled against television is that it makes children fat – turns them into 'telly tubbies', as a recent headline in the *Daily Mail* declared. The increase in childhood obesity became a serious concern in the nineties. A study conducted between 1996 and 1998 by Leeds Community and Mental Health Trust, involving 700 children in ten local primary schools, found that 15 per cent of seven- to eight-year-olds were overweight and 5 per cent were obese. Children's weight had increased 'frighteningly' over the last few decades, yet they were not eating much more than they did twenty or thirty years earlier. The key difference seemed to be lack of exercise. Another study, undertaken by Liverpool University and the West Hertfordshire Health Authority, examined more than 50,000 babies and children under four. It found that by 1998 23.6 per cent of children under four were overweight, compared to 14.7 per cent of pre-schoolers in 1989. The research team, led by Peter Bundred, Reader in Primary Care at the University of Liverpool, seemed stunned by its own findings. 'We knew that teenagers have become fatter, but for the first time we are seeing rapid increases in weight throughout the childhood years,' said Dr Bundred. 'The problem with toddlers is that we now have a situation where many mothers work, come home and need to do the housework so sit their children in front of a television or video.'[14]

It should be remembered, however, that parents' fear for their children's safety may have more to do with the children's relative inactivity than the hypnotic power of the box in the corner. Fear of paedophiles and psychopaths who might traumatize or seriously harm children has reached epidemic proportions. My own youngest granddaughter is not allowed to go out after four o'clock over the long dark winter months, so she either sits motionless at her desk doing homework or she lies on the living-room carpet watching television. Strenuous callisthenics over the weekend have kept the bulges under control, but this means that her parents' limited free time at the weekend is taken up with chauffeuring duties. The ball has in fact landed squarely in the parental court. Parents will have to screen, censor, discuss, choose and oversee the programmes their children watch, and they will have to balance passive viewing with plenty of carefully supervised exercise.

The sexual content of television programmes has become another worry. Should parents jump up nervously and switch off the set the moment a couple starts to simulate love-making (which often happens at weekends when children are allowed to stay up after the watershed)? Parents themselves can suffer embarrassment, as a Broadcasting Standards Council study found. One middle-aged father complained to the Council's interviewer candidly: 'You just don't feel right if you are sitting with your daughter and they start humping on the screen.'[15] Children's reactions to adult sexuality range from the fascinated to the timorous to the crude. Some children feel very uneasy at the sight of unbridled coupling in a sitcom or adult drama, especially when they are watching with their parents. One child interviewed by the BSC said that the sight triggered off visions of her parents making love. 'You don't like to think of your parents having sex,' she said, 'because they're your parents and you see them as protectors . . . as making the dinner.'[16]

Combined family viewing can raise other problems. I recall how terrified my older grandchild, Maisie, was when an episode of *East-Enders* in the late eighties contained a rape scene. We did not see the rape, which took place in a park, but heard the victim's blood-curdling screams. No warning had been broadcast. 'What's happened to her? Why is she screaming?' Maisie kept asking. It was impossible to explain what was happening to a kindergarten-aged child who had previously loved cycling in her local park. She refused to go there for weeks afterwards.

So, yes, television is full of snares. It can spring unsuitable material on innocent minds; it can confuse and contort parents' wish to be candid with their offspring about sexuality and its darker aspects. Looking back over the past fifty years, one would have to concede that the 'box of delights' has not been an unmixed blessing. But there is no reason to be despondent. It is encouraging to recognize that children's television *does* impart knowledge, it is both entertaining and instructive.

Most hopeful of all, perhaps, television does not invade a child's mind to the exclusion of all other creative activities. As Hilde Himmelweit wrote, television's supposed 'halo effect', meaning that it is more appealing and enchanting than any other activity, has proved to be an illusion. She concluded that 'children reach satiation point in their desire for a consumption of ready-made entertainment. They will sit and watch or listen, for a given time and no more.'[17] Children can and do switch off the plug-in drug. The twentieth-century scaremongers did not accurately foretell the future of television in children's lives. It has a secure place in their daily routines but not a stranglehold.

Notes

Chapter 1: Early Years

1. Tom Sinclair, 'Howdy Doody', in *The 100 Greatest TV Shows of All Time*, Time Inc., New York, 1998.
2. The Colindale Newspaper Library of the British Library carries two broadsheets of the last century's daily news: *The Times* and the *Daily Express*. I have concentrated on the *Daily Express* because of its emphasis on entertainment; it was also brilliant under its then editor Arthur Christiansen.
3. D. Buckingham, H. Davies, K. Jones and P. Kelley, *Children's Television in Britain*, British Film Institute, London, 1999.
4. Anna Home, *Into the Box of Delights*, BBC Books, London, 1993.
5. The BBC's *Watch with Mother* compilation, released in 1998, had made £4 million by the end of 1999.
6. Bob Monkhouse, *Crying with Laughter*, Arrow Books, London, 1993, p. 208.
7. Betty Friedan, *The Feminine Mystique*, W.W. Norton, New York, 1963.
8. Buckingham et al., op. cit., p. 21.
10. Home, op. cit., p. 35.

Chapter 2: The Sixties

1. Newton N. Minow and Craig L. Lamay, *Abandoned in the Wasteland: Children's Television and the First Amendment*, Hill and Wang, New York, 1995, p.199.
2. Quoted in Buckingham et al., op. cit.
3. 'Why TV chief hired American', *Daily Express*, 20 October 1962.
4. Quoted in Buckingham et al., op. cit.

5. Ibid.

6. *Inside BBC Television: A Year Behind the Camera*, introduced by Richard Baker, Webb and Bower, London, 1983.

7. Lynn Barber, 'Drag Queen', *Observer Magazine*, 30 January 2000.

8. Denis Foreman, *Persona Granada*, André Deutsch, London, 1997.

9. F.B. Rainsberry, *A History of Children's Television in English Canada, 1952–1986*, Scarecrow Press, Metuchen, NJ, and London, 1988.

10. Monica Sims writing in November 1971 issue of *Voice and Vision* magazine.

11. Buckingham et al., op cit.

12. Peter Haining, *Dr Who: The Time Travellers' Guide*, W.H. Allen, London, 1987.

13. Until 1978, when it created a special archival library in Windmill Lane, London, the BBC had no proper place for storing the *Dr Who* tapes. Some 109 sixties' *Dr Who* tapes were either junked or burnt – one of the great creative disasters of entertainment history. Lack of money was blamed for this destruction. Another reason is that the London Fire Brigade deemed them a fire hazard. Fans sometimes rub salt into their own wounds by listing lost episodes on cult websites. One online anecdote tells of a producer in the early seventies reaching into his desk and taking out a sliced strip of celluloid to pick at his back molars. It was from a *Dr Who* can.

14. Actress Carole Ann Ford played the part of Susan. Sexier actresses starred later on in the series, notably Joan Collins and Kate O'Mara.

15. The seven Doctors were played by: William Hartnell, 1963–6; Patrick Troughton, 1966–9; Jon Pertwee, 1969–73; Tom Baker, 1974–80; Peter Davison, 1980–84; Colin Baker, 1984–6; and Sylvester McCoy, 1986–96. An eighth Doctor, Paul McGann, appeared in a one-off television movie in 1996.

16. Simon Archer and Stan Nicholls, *Gerry Anderson: The Authorised Biography*, Orbit, London, 1998.

17. Mark Phillips, 'The History of TV's *Lost in Space* (Part One)', www.lostinspacetv.com/NEWS/history1.html.

18. Stephen E. Whitfield and Gene Roddenberry, *The Making of Star Trek*, Ballantine Books, New York, 1968.

19. Archer and Nicholls, op cit.

20. Ibid., p. 72.

21. Ibid.

22. Matthew Bond, 'Master of Telling TV Tales', Arts and Books Section, *Daily Telegraph*, 24 July 1999.
23. Delgado died tragically in a UK traffic accident in 1973, a shock for fans.
24. 'Clangers in *Dr Who*', www.clangers.co.uk/drwho.htm.

Chapter 3: The Seventies
1. Buckingham et al., op. cit.
2. The late Joe Barbera and Bill Hanna themselves deny that the mouse, Jerry, is a victim, stating in their biography (Michael Mallory, *Hanna-Barbera Cartoons*, Hugh Lauter Levin Associates, Hong Kong, 1998): 'Although he is frequently menaced by Tom, he [Jerry] is anything but a victim . . . no other cartoon character is quite as resourceful in defending himself with a mallet, fruit pie, frying pan, tennis racquet, or whatever else is handy.'
3. Minow and Lamay, op. cit.
4. Ibid.
5. Buckingham et al., op. cit.
6. Home, op. cit.
7. Ibid.
8. John Nathan, *Sony – The Private Life*, Houghton Mifflin, New York, NY, 1999.
9. In the brilliant seventies' novel by Roddy Doyle, *The Woman Who Walked Into Doors* (Penguin, Harmondsworth, 1996), the heroine's family sit around the television in Dublin watching *Catweazle*. Charlo, the husband-to-be, pronounces it 'brutal' (meaning 'bad'). He is the one who turns out to be brutal in the end, ironically.
10. Home, op. cit.
11. Mallory, op. cit.
12. For a more extensive analysis of this question, see Chapter 7.
13. Mark Phillips and Frank Garcia, *Science Fiction Television Series: Episode Guides, Histories and Casts and Credits for 62 Prime Time Shows, 1959 Through 1989*, McFarland and Co., Jefferson, NC, and London, 1996.
14. Buckingham et al., op. cit.
15. On the subject of the Sex Pistols, I should like to put in a plea here for my old friend the late Bill Grundy, who now seems to be remembered solely for his television interview with the scorchingly insulting group. Bill also wrote a brilliant book on Fleet Street called *The Press: Inside*

Out (W.H. Allen, London, 1976). I am not sure why a good book should be eclipsed by an embarrassing Thames Television interview show, but that is another story.

16. Frank Broughton (ed.), *Time Out: Interviews 1968–1998*, Penguin, Harmondsworth, 1998.

17. For more about reactions to *Grange Hill*, see Chapter 5.

Chapter 4: The Eighties

1. 'Step Back in Time from '99', Institute of Management news release, 6 May 1999, www.inst-mgt.org.uk/institute/press/trends.html.

2. Hugo Young, *One of Us: A Biography of Margaret Thatcher*, Macmillan, London, 1989.

3. Roland Rat was the brainchild of children's producer Anne Wood, who worked with children's programmes on TV-am. However, she was not the rodent's creator. She went on to create *Teletubbies* for the BBC in 1996.

4. Michael Leapman, *Treachery? The Power Struggle at TV-am*, Allen and Unwin, London, 1984.

5. Perhaps the best-known example of this debate in the UK concerned the killing of two-year-old James Bulger in February 1993 by the boys Jon Venables and Robert Thompson. They had watched the horror video *Child's Play 3*, in which a hideous doll is seen committing crimes. However, no causal relationship was established between the film and the crime.

6. C. Atkins, B.S. Greenberg, F. Korzenny and S. McDermott, 'Selective Exposure to Televised Violence', *Journal of Broadcasting*, Vol. 21, 1979, pp. 5–12.

7. Russ Laczniak, 'Action Figures Draw Fire', *Iowa Stater* (reported from Iowa State University campus bulletin), 15 December 1995.

8. Working with children in groups on *Magpie* served Marilyn Gaunt well. In the spring of 2002 she won the BAFTA award for Best Documentary with her delicate film of four sisters living in barely tolerable council squalor in the Midlands, entitled *Kelly and Her Sisters*. The documentary also netted two other awards: the Broadcast Award and the Royal Television Society Award.

9. Roald Dahl, *George's Marvellous Medicine*, Jonathan Cape, London, 1981.

10. Ted Hughes, *The Iron Man*, Faber and Faber, London, 1985.

Chapter 5: The Nineties

1. Rosemarie Jarski, *Hollywood Wit*, Prion Books, London, 2000.
2. Quoted in Buckingham et al., op. cit.
3. Ruth Inglis, *Sins of the Fathers: A Study of the Physical and Emotional Abuse of Children*, Peter Owen, London, 1978.
4. The nine o'clock 'watershed' is the agreed time that UK broadcasters, both commercial and public service, have set. Before this time no unsuitable sexual or violent content shall be aired. If the news is to show disturbing material beforehand, the announcers give well-timed prior warning.
5. Peter T. Kelly (ed.), *Television Violence: A Guide to the Literature*, Nova Science Publishers, Commack, NY, 1999.
6. The wisdom of legislating in favour of the V-chip was debated furiously in the US Congress throughout the nineties. President Clinton argued that it should be given first priority, but his advocacy fell on deaf ears. The Senate agreed only to place a limit on violent and sexual programming via the V-chip in September 2000. V-chip technology is now required by law in all new television sets thirteen inches and larger, with encoded ratings displayed on 'unsuitable' shows.
7. Marie Winn, *The Plug-In Drug*, Viking Penguin, London and New York, 1977.
8. Minow and Lamay, op. cit.
9. Quoted in *The Bulletin: The Jesuit Communication Project*, ed. John J. Pungente, East Ontario, Canada, 17 December 1996.
10. Broadcasting Standards Council, *Reviewing Children Viewing*, BSC, London, 1996.
11. Op. cit., note 9.
12. Ibid.
13. John Cain, *The BBC: Seventy Years of Broadcasting*, BBC Publications, London, 1992.
14. One bizarre objection did come in 1999 from the conservative American religious leader, the Reverend Jerry Falwell, who suggested angrily that the purple-clad, handbag-carrying Tinky Winky was promoting a 'gay lifestyle'.
15. Tiffany Daneff, 'Let's Go Gardening with the Teletubbies', *Saturday Telegraph*, 31 May 1997.
16. Ruki Sayed, 'Making a Fortune Is Child's Play', *Daily Mirror*, 4 January 2001.

17. Victor Lewis-Smith, 'The Explicit Flowerpot Men', *Evening Standard*, 5 January 2001.
18. Kate Taylor, quoted in Carol Iaciofano and Don Aucoin, 'Hey, Mom, Can I Watch TV?', *Boston Globe*, Sunday 16 December 1998.
19. Buckingham et al., op. cit.
20. Hilde Himmelweit, A.N. Oppenheim and Pamela Vince, *Television and the Child*, Oxford University Press, Oxford, 1958.
21. This bit of repartee was provided by writer Tom Congdon in *Forbes Magazine*, 12 November 2000, in a feature on pantomime.
22. www.dangermouse.org/what.html.
23. Alex Lesman, 'Yellow Trash', http/xroads.virginia.edu/~MA96/lesman/thesis.html.
24. Jan Breslauer, *The Making of the Rugrats Movie*, Klasky Csupo Publishing, Hollywood, Calif., 1998.
25. Interviewed by Kevin Macdonald in *Projections Five*, 1996.
26. Home, op. cit.
27. Lenny Henry and Steve Parkhouse, *The Quest for the Big Woof*, Penguin, Harmondsworth, 1991.

Chapter 6: From Bagpuss to Big Business

1. Oliver Postgate, *Seeing Things: An Autobiography*, Sidgwick and Jackson, 2000, p. 295.
2. Ibid., p. 265.
3. http://www.marklitwak.com/movmerc.html.
4. Norma Odom Pecora, *The Business of Children's Entertainment*, Guildford Press, Hove, 1998, p. 55.
5. G. Wayne Miller, *Toy Wars: The Epic Struggle Between GI Joe, Barbie and the Companies That Make Them*, Times Books, New York, 1998, p. xiii.
6. Dan S. Acuff, *What Kids Buy and Why*, Free Press, New York, 1997, p. 63.
7. *Observer Magazine*, 26 November 2000.
8. The tradition of really stupid ideas continues to this day, with Hasbro again taking the lead. In April 2001 Hasbro announced that it was developing a computer game called 'Pox', which would pit youngsters against a deadly alien virus. Similarly euphonious names were found in other aisles of the local toy store: parents were quaking at the imminent arrival of the Butt-Ugly Martians, who love to scoff popcorn and hang around shopping malls, among other ennobling pastimes.

The Butt-Ugly Martians is produced by the Derbyshire-based Just Group, who made *Pinky and Perky*.

9. Miller, op. cit., pp. 25–6.

10. Pecora, op. cit., pp. 41–2.

11. *Time*, 9 April 2001 (European edition).

12. *Observer Magazine*, 26 November 2000.

13. Cain, op. cit., p. 118.

14. Marie Winn, *The Plug-In Drug: Television, Children and the Family*, Penguin, Harmondsworth, 1985, p. 128.

15. Edward L. Palmer and Aimee Dorr (eds), *Children and the Faces of Television: Teaching, Violence, Selling*, Academic Press, New York, 1980.

16. James U. McNeal, *Kids as Customers: A Handbook of Marketing to Children*, Lexington Books, New York, 1992, p. 91; James U. McNeal, *The Kids' Market: Myths and Realities*, Paramount Market Publishing, Ithaca, NY, 1999, p. 30.

17. *Sunday Times*, 22 April 2001.

18. *Forbes*, 22 January 2001.

19. Although ostensibly free from sexual references, *Bob the Builder* has become an icon for some adults, regarded (according to one survey) as more sexually attractive than football player David Beckham.

20. Pecora, op. cit., p. 76.

21. *New York Times*, 13 May 2001.

22. Elissa Moses, *The $100 Billion Allowance: Assessing the Global Teen Market*, John Wiley and Sons, New York, NY, 2000, pp. 10–12.

23. I had to double-check the manufacturer's name, which shows that witty, creative advertisements do not necessarily stamp the all-important brand name on the viewer's mind. Advertisers themselves have grave doubts about the usefulness of 'funny' advertisements; and, most tellingly of all, the American Marketing Association bestows the EFFIE awards for commercials that are effective in getting results (not necessarily entertaining). 'EFFIE is dedicated to the notion that *the best advertising* is the advertising that does *the best job*' (www.effie.org).

24. The fellow who portrayed the thirsty lemonade addict in the original commercials later ran off to a kibbutz in Israel, according to the *Sunday Times*, 30 April 2000.

25. *Sunday Times*, 30 April 2000. Voiceovers fulfil a slightly different function in the USA, where famous actors are employed because the public holds them in great affection. Voiceovers have certain

advantages over on-camera appearances, especially for elderly actors who are perhaps no longer as in demand as they were (an important consideration in an ageist society); and such commercials are significantly cheaper to produce and coordinate.

26. May Kenworthy, the lady who modelled as 'Gloria' in the Ovaltine campaigns of the thirties, subsequently died by overdosing on barbiturates, somewhat detracting from the wholesomeness of the product's image.
27. Reprise Records, 1988.
28. Wilson Key, *Subliminal Seduction*, Signet Classics, 1973, p. 66.
29. Ibid., p. 156.
30. Quoted in Winn, op. cit., p. 12.
31. This article mentions the interesting fact that selling goods to children was punishable by death under the Hammurabi Code of 1750 BC.
32. Key, op. cit., pp. 158–9.
33. http://www.rebelmothers.org.
34. Politicians ignore this constituency at their peril, as President Clinton recognized when he targeted much clever politicking at the so-called 'soccer moms'.
35. Winn, op. cit., p. 214.
36. Quoted in Ruth Inglis, *A Time to Learn*, Peter Owen, London, 1973.
37. http://www.lionlamb.org.
38. *Skeptical Inquirer*, May/June 2001.
39. *New York Times*, 20 January 2001.
40. Sheryl Leach, a Texan, created him with her two-year-old son in mind and produced home videos at her father-in-law's video business: *Washington Post*, 13 September 1993.
41. Ibid.
42. Pecora, op. cit., p. 108. PBS did not always do so badly, however. By 1998 PBS was getting 'an undisclosed cut of *Teletubbies*-related sales. It received $3.5 million in proceeds from total sales of licensed products the latest fiscal year, in which its budget was $247 million. The money is used to be additional programming, PBS says.' *USA Today*, 27 October 1998.
43. The original *Lost in Space* inspired intense loyalty, partly because of its emphasis on family relationships and characters one could care about. But the show's producers also cleverly ensured that viewers would return week after week by giving each episode a trademark cliffhanger ending – you had to tune in next week to see how things would turn out.

44. Postgate, op. cit., p. 276.
45. http://www.jewishsf.com/bk980417/etsesame.html.
46. *The Times* (online edition), 14 May 2001. The website is http://www.bbc.co.uk/treasurehunt. Wendy Richard later went on to fame in *Are You Being Served?* and, more recently, *EastEnders*.
47. *New York Times*, 29 April 2001.
48. 'The Flintstones', *USA Today*, 29 April 1994.
49. Audrey Geisel, the formidable widow of *Cat-in-the-Hat* creator Theodor Seuss Geisel, is much less amenable to suggestions for changes to the original and uses the full power of copyright law to ensure that Dr Seuss is not tampered with. Even Steven Spielberg must bow to her will. 'The licensing enterprise was formed not to capitalize on Ted's work but to guard it,' she has said (*Forbes*, 20 March 2000).
50. *New York Times*, 3 June 2001.
51. *Pediatrics*, June 2001.
52. Victor Lewis-Smith, *Evening Standard*, 5 January 2001. He raises an interesting question. What exactly is the source and nature of the Daleks' evil? It could come from the 'Dalek Invasion of Earth', which explicitly likened the Daleks to Nazis, with their imprisonment of captive populations in camps, and of course their emphasis on extermination.

Chapter 7: The Emotional Effects of Television on Children

1. *Washington Journalism Review*, October 1989.
2. Edmund L. Andrews, 'Laws, Guidelines and Standards', in Kelly, op. cit., p. 237.
3. Ibid.
4. Ellen Seiter, *Television and New Media Audiences*, Oxford University Press, Oxford, 1999.
5. Palmer and Dorr, op. cit.
6. Hilde T. Himmelweit, A.N. Oppenheim and Pamela Vince, *Television and the Child*, Oxford University Press, Oxford, 1958.
7. Ibid.
8. Kelly, op. cit.
9. Seiter, op. cit.
10. Quoted in Steve Wulf, 'TV or Not TV', www.time.com/time/magazine/1997/dom/970908/fam.tvornottv.html.

11. Kelly, op. cit.
12. Ibid.
13. David Buckingham and Mark Allerton, *Fear, Fright and Distress: A Review of Research on Children's 'Negative' Emotional Responses to Television*, Working Paper 12, Broadcasting Standards Council, London, 1996.
14. Nigel Hawkes, 'The Telly-Tubby Toddlers Who Get Fat on TV Diet', www.heartlink.org.uk/headlines2001/july2001/10th-july-2001/headlines10.html.
15. Andrea Millwood Hargrave, *Sex and Sexuality in Broadcasting*, Broadcasting Standards Council, London, 1992.
16. Ibid.
17. Himmelweit et al., op. cit.

Index

n = endnote (indexed only for background information, not simple citations)